TANGLED ENTANGLED : GEN Z

DECODING THE TWIST OF A GENERATION WIRED FOR CHANGE

MAHBOOB ALAM

This book is dedicated to the true Gen Z—those born after 2000 in my definition, like myself, who are navigating this fast-paced, ever-evolving world. To the dreamers, the doers, and the challengers of norms, this is for you. As a 20-year-old Gen Z, I dedicate these words to our restless energy, our impatience for change, and our unique way of shaping the future. Let's continue to redefine boundaries and create a world where our voice is heard.

....

Contents

Foreword

In an era defined by rapid change and innovation, the voice of Gen Z is more vital than ever. "Tangled Entangled : Gen Z" captures the essence of a generation navigating the complexities of modern life, blending the urgency of youth with profound insights into the challenges we face. This book serves as a bridge between generations, offering perspectives that foster understanding and empathy.

Through candid storytelling and thought-provoking reflections, the author invites readers to embark on a journey that highlights the resilience, creativity, and adaptability of Gen Z. As we delve into the pages ahead, we are not just witnessing a narrative but engaging with a movement poised to shape the future.

May this book inspire dialogue and connection, helping us all appreciate the rich tapestry of experiences that define our world today.

Preface

A story of Mind

Acknowledgements

Writing this book has been a journey full of learning and growth, and I am deeply grateful to everyone who supported me along the way.

First and foremost, I want to thank my family for their constant encouragement and belief in me. To my sisters, Sophia and Ahmadi, your love and support have been a source of strength throughout this process. My pillar Ziaullah khan , and I couldn't have done this without you.

A special thanks to my friend Jaskaran, who offered valuable insights and perspectives that shaped much of this book. Moreover to all my friends for ideas and conversations helped me see things in a new light, and I'm deeply appreciative of your friendship.

To all my friends and family, your encouragement and belief in me have made this book possible. Thank you for being a part of this journey!

Prologue

Gen Z—often labeled as the digital generation, the impatient ones, or the disruptors—carries more than just a love for technology. We live in a time of rapid change, navigating life through screens, ideas, and experiences faster than ever before. This book isn't just about the challenges we face; it's about how we, a generation born after 2000, think, adapt, and redefine everything we touch.

As I write this, I'm not just telling my story, but also reflecting on what makes us unique—the push for purpose, the pursuit of passions, and the struggle with societal expectations. In this tangled, often confusing world, we're finding our way, and this book is a glimpse into that journey. You may find **contradictions** within the book itself, but again that what a Gen Z is.

Welcome to the world of Gen Z, seen through the eyes of one of its own.

Introduction

In a world where change is the only constant, Gen Z has grown up navigating an unprecedented landscape shaped by rapid technological advancements and global disruptions. From the dawn of the internet era to the drastic shifts brought by the COVID-19 pandemic, and into a post-pandemic world, our generation has faced a whirlwind of change that has fundamentally influenced how we think, act, and relate to the world.

I'll never forget the day when the pandemic turned our lives upside down. I was in the middle of and suddenly, everything changed. This moment, among many others, has shaped my perspective and taught me valuable lessons about adaptability, resilience, and understanding. These personal experiences, along with the stories of my friends and family, will guide us through the complexities of mind.

Our lives have been marked by a relentless pace of transformation, from the early days of the internet to the social upheavals and economic uncertainties that followed. This book aims to offer a window into the complex mindset of Gen Z. We are often misunderstood, labeled as impatient or disconnected, but our experiences tell a different story. Our generation is not defined by immaturity but by the unique ways we adapt to a world that is constantly evolving. Through my personal journey and the narratives of those around me, I will explore how these dynamic changes have shaped our perspectives and behaviors. By delving into the highs and lows of our experiences, I hope to provide insights into the nature of our generation and encourage a deeper understanding from previous generations. Sound interesting hmm? Let's see.

I invite you to join me on this journey, to explore the challenges we face and the ways we have learned to cope and thrive. This book is not just about explaining our mindset but also about fostering empathy and bridging the generational divide. My hope is that by the end, readers will gain a clearer understanding of the Gen Z experience and appreciate the diverse ways we navigate this ever-changing world.

ONE
GROWING UP

Growing up as a Gen Z kid in Patna, Bihar, my childhood seemed ordinary at first glance. I lived in a joint family, surrounded by many siblings, which naturally turned me into an extrovert. Attending Radiant International School, a well-known institution in my hometown, I remember my first day vividly. Much to my surprise, I was appointed as the class monitor. It was a proud moment, my first taste of responsibility, and a sign of the small but meaningful milestones that would follow.

From an early age, I was the entertainer among my friends, known for my mimicry, beatboxing, and cracking jokes. I had a large circle, but only a few close friends stuck by my side. Those friendships would become valuable later, offering support as I navigated the whirlwind of adolescence. Little did I know how crucial those bonds would be in helping me tackle the challenges that lay ahead. As I hit 7th grade, life started to change. It wasn't just me; everything around me felt different too. I recall my English teacher's parting advice at the end of 6th grade: "You'll have wings now, but don't fly too high. Focus on your studies ..it's only going to get tougher." She wasn't wrong. The academic pressure ramped up, and so did our rebellious streaks. We started pushing boundaries, questioning teachers, exploring relationships, and using our appearances as a form of self-expression.

One time, I decided to get a trendy spiked haircut, thinking it would be my moment to shine. But as soon as I stepped onto the school grounds, the gatekeeper stopped me in my tracks.... my hairstyle was deemed "inappropriate." While that day was a small setback, it didn't kill my spirit. My Social Studies teacher even made me stand in front of the class and explain how I got that haircut. I loved expressing myself through my looks, and soon, I became known for my stylish, often unconventional hairstyles. Sports were another passion of mine, particularly kabaddi. The success of the Patna Pirates in the Pro Kabaddi League fueled my excitement. However, while I had the enthusiasm, my skills didn't quite match up. So, I shifted my focus to something else "beatboxing" . I honed this craft using YouTube tutorials, carefully rationing my 3GB monthly data to master the art.

Speaking of data, the year 2016 was a turning point. Back then, having 3GB of data for the whole month was a luxury. You'd have to plan your online activities wisely. But then came Jio, with its game-changing free data packages. Suddenly, unlimited internet access was in our hands, transforming our generation's experience. Ambani ji deserves special mention here!

The advent of unlimited internet reshaped our ecosystem. We no longer felt confined by our location or resources. Suddenly, we had access to a global network of ideas, trends, and cultures, connecting us in ways we couldn't have imagined. We explored the endless world of the internet, learned new skills, and immersed ourselves in the digital age like never before. As I grew older, my interests began to shift more toward the digital world. I remember the first time I stumbled across digital marketing was like discovering a new universe. Watching brands and businesses thrive online, connecting with customers, and leveraging the power of social media fascinated me. With Jio's unlimited internet, I spent countless hours watching YouTube tutorials on everything from graphic design to social media marketing.

It wasn't long before I started experimenting with what I learned in our family business, a hotel. I took over the social media marketing, ran ad campaigns, and watched as we started to see results. The instant feedback from the digital world felt tailor-made for my Gen Z mindset... an ad, get immediate reactions. That instant gratification hit the spot. Yet, looking back, I sometimes wonder if I made the right academic choices. My sister had advised me to choose science in school, envisioning a future where tech and engineering were king. But at the time, I wasn't drawn to it. Commerce seemed cool, and I made that decision in typical Gen Z style quickly, without much deliberation.

It's funny how we Gen Zs operate. We're action-oriented; we make decisions fast. But afterward, we tend to overthink. "What if I had taken science? Would I be deep into tech now? Could I be coding or building the next big app?" These thoughts sometimes flood my mind. We jump into decisions, then later, we can't stop spinning the "What if?" wheel.

That said, I don't entirely regret my path. Learning digital marketing has given me an edge. It allowed me to bring something fresh to the family business, something no one else in my circle could. I got to see real-time results from my efforts, something a traditional classroom couldn't teach me. But yes, there are moments when I think, "If only I had listened to my sister and gone the science route." This is a core Gen Z trait... we lack patience for what doesn't feel right in the moment, but later, we're left dealing with a little FOMO.

So this brings me to say, though, it's just who we are. We act fast, we learn fast, and yes, sometimes we overthink. But that's part of the Gen Z journey. We're constantly balancing the thrill of living in the moment with the lingering "What if?" doubts. And honestly, I wouldn't have it any other way.

TWO

HUSTLE

In a world that revolves around clicks, likes, shares, and impressions, Gen Z has grown up with an inherent need for validation that goes far beyond the classroom or family circle. From Instagram's 'like' button to TikTok's 'for you' page, social media platforms have redefined what it means to be seen, heard, and valued. For Gen Z, who have never known a world without these digital platforms, the search for validation is more intense than ever before. It's as if every selfie, every post, every interaction needs to be validated with numbers, proving that we matter, that our voices are important, and that we are, indeed, "cool , shi h bro."

This habit of seeking validation isn't merely a byproduct of teenage insecurity but a deeply embedded part of the social media ecosystem. Social media platforms thrive on engagement likes, shares, comments, and impressions and they've subtly trained our brains to crave these interactions as signs of approval. It's not just the dopamine hit we get from each 'like'; it's the underlying affirmation that we are good enough, interesting enough, or attractive enough. This leads to a culture where even our most authentic moments are staged, filtered, and curated for maximum engagement.

I remember my friend, let's call him orry , who embodied this validation-seeking behavior perfectly. Orry was the quintessential 'cool guy' in our group or at least, that's what he wanted everyone to think. Every joke he cracked was aimed at seeking approval, particularly from the girls in our class. He'd constantly make fun of his male friends, often at their expense, just to appear humorous and gain popularity among the opposite gender. It didn't matter if his jokes were hurtful or embarrassing; all that mattered to him was that the girls found him entertaining. Orry believed that his worth was tied to how 'cool' or 'funny' he appeared to others, and social media only amplified this. When Instagram became popular, Orry's behavior took a new turn. His feed was full of pictures with female friends, each one carefully crafted to give off the 'play boy' vibe. He thought this validated him as someone who was desirable, popular, and above all, worth noticing. The funny thing is, all of us, his close friends, could see right through it.

We knew who Orry really was... a good guy with deep insecurities. He wasn't a player; he just wanted to be seen as one because that's what he thought the world expected from him. This is the dangerous side of the validation-seeking habit. It creates a false identity that may earn likes and shares but leaves the individual feeling hollow and disconnected from their true self.

The Pressure to be 'Perfect'

Orry's story is not unique. I've seen many of my peers struggling with the same need to create an online persona that matches society's ideals of success, beauty, and popularity. And it's not just limited to the 'cool guy' image; for others, it's about crafting the perfect lifestyle. You'll see them posting their gym routines, curated outfits, or holiday destinations images that scream "I'm living my best life." It's a cycle that many of us fall into, where we're not just living our lives but constantly seeking **external validation** for it. Gen Z's obsession with validation isn't just anecdotal. Research has shown that the need for social validation is more prominent in Gen Z than in any other generation. A 2019 study by the Pew Research Center found that 72% of teens and young adults reported feeling pressure to be 'popular' on social media. Another report by Common Sense Media in 2021 revealed that 70% of Gen Z users believe social media negatively impacts their self-esteem, with the majority citing the pressure to present a perfect life online.

And you can see it in everything from #sunkissed selfies to motivational captions under every post. Even our most genuine moments are filtered and edited to match the online aesthetics that everyone else seems to be living. But what happens when we don't get the validation we expect? What happens when a post doesn't perform as well, when those likes don't roll in? I've seen people delete posts that didn't get 'enough' engagement within an hour or two because, somehow, it doesn't feel real unless it's validated by others.

The quest for validation goes beyond just posting pictures or getting likes. For Gen Z, validation often determines how they feel about themselves. Whether it's getting enough likes on an Instagram post or receiving positive feedback on a YouTube video, these small digital affirmations accumulate into a broader sense of **self-worth**. If they don't receive the validation they expect, it can lead to feelings of inadequacy, anxiety, and even depression.

Logic behind 'Validation-Seeking'

This is a phenomenon rooted in the way our brains react to social media. Studies from the University of California, Los Angeles (UCLA) have found that receiving likes on social media activates the same reward center in the brain that is triggered by winning money or eating chocolate. (" I know you might be thinking why this heavy facts has been put in between, don't worry I'll not through much") . It's a dopamine rush, and just like with any addictive behavior, we crave more of it. The more likes we get, the more validated we feel, and conversely, the fewer likes we get, the more rejected we feel. This instant feedback loop keeps Gen Z coming back for more, fueling the cycle of validation-seeking behavior.

When this validation is absent, the consequences can be severe. Gen Z has some of the highest reported rates of anxiety and depression among all age groups, and much of this is linked to the pressure to fit in, both online and offline. In a 2020 survey conducted by the American Psychological Association, nearly 91% of Gen Z individuals reported experiencing some form of physical or emotional stress due to social media use. Many of them pointed to the constant comparison with others as a significant factor contributing to their mental health struggles. When Orry's posts didn't get as many likes as he expected, or when his jokes didn't land with the girls, you could see the shift in his behavior. He'd withdraw, become moody, and even lash out at friends for no apparent reason. It was as if the lack of external validation stripped him of his self-worth, leaving him questioning whether he was good enough. And Orry isn't alone in this. Across the world, young people are grappling with the emotional fallout of not meeting the unrealistic standards set by social media.

The Role of 'Fake Identities'

One of the most concerning aspects of this validation-seeking behavior is the rise of 'fake identities' on social media. Orry's case is a perfect example of this. On Instagram, he carefully curated his persona as a charming, carefree, 'cool guy,' but in reality, he was struggling with insecurity and self-doubt. Social media allows people to create idealized versions of themselves, which may earn them more validation but at the cost of their **authentic-self.**

Nowadays many of young adults between the ages of 16 and 24 admitted to exaggerating or faking parts of their life on social media to receive more attention or validation. These fake personas can lead to feelings of loneliness and alienation because, deep down, these individuals know that the validation they're receiving isn't for who they truly are.

Overthinking and Fast 'Decisions'

The need for validation can quickly spiral into an unhealthy obsession. When Gen Z doesn't receive the validation they're seeking, they may fall into a cycle of overthinking. This is where the paradox of Gen Z comes into play they make quick decisions but often overthink the outcomes when those decisions don't lead to the validation they expected.

For example, I often think back to my decision to choose Commerce over Science in high school. At the time, I made the choice quickly, thinking it was the right move. But over the years,

I've questioned that decision endlessly. What if I had chosen Science? Would I have learned more about technology, something that fascinates me now? Would I be better off in my career? This overthinking often stems from the fact that we didn't receive immediate validation for our decisions, causing us to doubt ourselves in the long run. In a world where every post, every story, every tweet carries the weight of how it will be perceived, Gen Z often finds themselves at a crossroads between being authentic and being "liked." Social media, which started as a platform for genuine expression and connection, has morphed into a complex arena where identity becomes a product, a curated image designed for maximum impact. The line between real and staged, between our true selves and our online personas, has blurred beyond recognition.

Authenticity is something that we, as a generation, claim to value deeply. You'll hear Gen Z talk about being "real" all the time. We say we want to be authentic, to present ourselves as we are, flaws and all. But here's the paradox.... being "real" online is often performative in itself. How often do we share our unfiltered thoughts, our raw emotions, without wondering how they'll be received? How often do we post photos of ourselves when we don't look our best, or when we're not feeling confident? Rarely, if ever (some on pvt. account with just close circle) . This is where the hustle for validation becomes a kind of trap. On one hand, we want to be true to ourselves. On the other, we want the world to recognize, approve of, and "like" that truth. But social media, with its algorithms and endless streams of filtered perfection, rarely rewards raw authenticity. The posts that get the most attention, the most likes, the most shares are often the ones that are polished, idealized, and, yes, sometimes inauthentic.

Take Orry, for instance, a friend whose digital persona was as meticulously crafted as a celebrity's brand. Orry, who was deeply insecure about his appearance, always posted pictures that were carefully angled, edited, and filtered to portray him as effortlessly cool. His captions were witty, his outfits on point, his vibe chill but the reality behind the screen was different. Orry spent hours obsessing over each post, overthinking the timing, the hashtags, the engagement. When he didn't get the validation he craved when his posts didn't rack up enough likes or when his followers didn't respond the way he hoped, he spiraled into doubt and anxiety. I think if he wouldn't have thought about anyone's opinion, he was perfect.

The thing is, Orry wasn't alone in this. Most of us, at one point or another, have been there agonizing over which version of ourselves to present, which facet of our lives to share. We've spent more time than we'd like to admit staging our "candid" moments, perfecting our "effortless" look, all for the sake of those few extra likes. And we justify it, saying we're just "playing the game" because everyone else is doing it. But what happens when we lose sight of who we are underneath all the filters?

The Illusion of 'Perfection'

One of the reasons authenticity feels so difficult to achieve in the social media age is the pervasive illusion of perfection. On platforms like Instagram, Snapchat, and TikTok, we're constantly bombarded with images of people living their "best lives." They're vacationing in exotic places, wearing the trendiest clothes, working out in picture-perfect gyms, and eating the most photogenic food. But what we often forget is that these images are curated to show only the highlights the moments of joy, success, and glamour.

The comparison game is inevitable. Even when we know that what we see on social media isn't the full picture, it's hard not to feel inadequate when our own lives don't match up. This creates an insidious cycle: we start to believe that in order to be valued, we need to live up to these impossibly high standards. And so, we filter, edit, and stage our lives, hoping to project an image that fits the mold of perfection. It's not that we're lying about our lives; it's that we're selectively presenting the parts that we think will earn us the most validation. But here's the catch... no one's life is perfect, not even the influencers or celebrities we admire. Behind every perfectly curated feed is a human being with insecurities, struggles, and doubts. The illusion of perfection is just that an illusion. Yet, it's an illusion we're all complicit in perpetuating, whether we realize it or not.

Despite the overwhelming pressure to present a polished, perfect image, there's a growing movement within Gen Z to seek out real, authentic connections. We're tired of the superficiality, the constant hustle for validation. We crave genuine relationships both online and offline that allow us to be our true selves, without the need to perform.

In many ways, this search for authenticity has fueled the rise of platforms like BeReal, where the whole point is to capture spontaneous, unfiltered moments of your day. The platform encourages users to post without filters or staging, giving them just a two-minute window to snap a photo, no matter what they're doing. It's a small rebellion against the carefully curated lives we see elsewhere on social media. And for many, it's a breath of fresh air. But even on platforms like BeReal, the need for validation lingers. After all, we're still sharing these moments with others. We still want people to like what they see, even if it's "real." So the question remains.... can we ever truly escape the validation trap, or are we destined to seek approval in one form or another, no matter the platform?

Authenticity in the 'Age of Algorithms'

There's another layer to this issue that often goes unnoticed: the role of algorithms. Social media platforms are designed to show us what will keep us engaged, which often means prioritizing content that is polished, popular, and likely to generate high levels of interaction. The more likes, shares, and comments a post gets, the more likely it is to be seen by others. This creates a feedback loop where only certain types of content usually the most curated and staged to rise to the top, while more authentic, less polished posts get buried. As a result, even when we try to be real, the platform itself may not reward us for it. Authenticity doesn't always translate into high engagement, and for a generation that has grown up measuring their worth in likes and followers, this can be disheartening. It's hard to stay true to yourself when the algorithm seems to favor a more polished, filtered version of who you are.

So where does that leave us? How do we balance the need for validation with the desire to be authentic? It's not an easy question to answer, and it's one that Gen Z will likely grapple with for years to come. But perhaps the first step is recognizing that authenticity doesn't need to be perfect. Being real means embracing the messy, unfiltered, and sometimes awkward parts of life and being okay with the fact that not everyone will like it.

Ultimately, the hustle for validation is something we all experience, but it doesn't have to define us. We can learn to validate ourselves, independent of the likes, comments, and shares. We can strive to be authentic, not because it's trendy or because it will earn us more followers, but because it's how we stay true to ourselves in a world that constantly tells us to be someone else.

THREE

WE SMARTPHONE

Alright, so picture this: you're scrolling through Instagram, answering a friend's DM, watching a quick reels tutorial on how to make 1k a day with Instagram, and also half-listening to your professor's voice in the background on Zoom. Chaotic, right? Well, for us, it's normal. It's not that we're distracted; we've just mastered the art of juggling multiple tasks. Think about it, Gen Z is basically a generation of walking smartphones with 10 tabs open in our brains. Just like our phones, which can run dozens of apps at once, we too have adapted to managing various tasks in our daily lives, seamlessly switching between them.

We've grown up with technology that's designed to be fast, efficient, and constantly connected. Smartphones, tablets, laptops they're all about helping us do more in less time, and we've inherited that. Everything from social media, online shopping, instant messaging, and even schoolwork is designed for multitasking. Our brains have rewired themselves to mirror this fast-paced, tech-driven world.

My millennial brother always says, "You guys can't focus on anything for more than five seconds," which is a common complaint from older generations. But what they don't get is that this isn't about a lack of focus; it's about how we focus differently. Gen Z has mastered the ability to do multiple things at once because that's what the world demands of us. We've grown up in an era where everything is at your fingertips, and we've adapted to process information quickly and efficiently.

We're like smartphones in human form, jumping from app to app, or in our case, task to task. And honestly, it's not just a skill it's a **survival mechanism**. In a world where things are moving faster than ever before, if you can't keep up, you get left behind. For us, multitasking isn't a challenge; it's just how we operate. It's how we're wired to handle the constant barrage of notifications, emails, social media updates, and everything else that demands our attention.

Let me give you an example. Remember that time in college when you had a project due, but your friend's birthday party was on the same weekend, and you also had an assignment deadline right after? That's when our multitasking brains kick into high gear. Did we crumble under the pressure? Nope. We went to the party, finished the project, and still managed to submit that assignment on time. If that doesn't scream "multitasking mastery," I don't know what does.

Millennials and don't even get me started on Boomers…. don't get it. They think multitasking means you can't concentrate on one thing at a time. But here's the truth: we can focus, we just do it differently. It's like when you're listening to a Spotify playlist while also checking out Instagram reels. You're doing both, but neither task is really taking away from the other. In fact, we thrive on this fast-paced rhythm, which is why we seem more adapted to this constantly moving world than older generations.

Just like smartphones are designed to switch seamlessly between different apps, Gen Z's brains are designed to switch between tasks. Let's not forget: smartphones are constantly updating themselves to perform better, handle more tasks, and work faster. Gen Z is the same way we're always evolving alongside the technology we use. For example, when smartphones upgraded to faster processors, we upgraded the way we process information too. We learned to digest large amounts of data in short bursts because that's how the digital world works now.

Think of Instagram reels or TikTok videos those short bursts of entertainment or information are designed for quick consumption. They give you what you need in under 60 seconds, and we've adapted to that speed. Our brains are getting trained to shift through information quickly, pick out the important bits, and move on. This is why older generations often say we have short attention spans. But is that really a bad thing? It's not that we can't focus; it's just that we do it faster and more efficiently than previous generations. We've been trained by the technology we use to get the most out of our time, and it's reshaping how we approach tasks and make decisions.

In this sense, smartphones and Gen Z aren't just tools and users; they're companions evolving together. Just like how a smartphone can handle multiple apps running at once without slowing down (or at least the good ones can), Gen Z can handle different tasks, jumping between schoolwork, social media, and personal commitments without breaking a sweat. It's not chaos; it's our form of order. We thrive in this fast-paced, interconnected environment because it's the one we were born into. If we were to slow down, we wouldn't just be uncomfortable; we'd be out of place in the world that's speeding up around us.

Our connection to technology has made us faster, more adaptable, and better at multitasking than any generation before us. And while older generations might see it as a flaw, for us, it's a strength. We're living in a world that's faster than ever, and we've adapted to keep pace with it.

Yes, we're fast decision-makers, but how do we balance it with deeper thinking? to see how we juggle speed with strategy, and why being like a smartphone isn't always a bad thing.

We're always doing something or more accurately, we're always doing many things at once. Some people see it and think it's messy or disorganized, but to us, it's just normal life. We jump between tasks the same way we hop between apps on our phones, but what's unique is that we're not just multitasking for the sake of it. We're doing it because it's essential for how we survive in this hyperconnected world. But, let's dig deeper. While it may seem like we're just skimming the surface of everything, the reality is more complicated. Multitasking is more than a survival mechanism for us it's a reflection of how we think, act, and, sometimes, how we struggle.

Picture this: it's 2000. The internet is still dial-up, and phones aren't **"smart"** yet. You wanted to send a text? Cool, that'll take about five minutes of pressing buttons, each letter requiring you to hit the same key multiple times. But by the time we, the Gen Z cohort, came around, the world had transformed into this supercharged tech haven where everything moves fast, quicker than the older generations could have ever imagined. We were born into a world of smartphones, lightning-fast Wi-Fi, and social media. In essence, speed isn't just something we value; it's all we know. I remember when it took nearly 30 mins to download any app and we thought it to be fast and see now, even 30 sec seems slow snail.

It's not that we **choose** to multitask. It's that the world we were born into demands it. Think about how many times you've had to reply to a text while writing an essay or even managing a work Zoom call while checking Instagram during the boring parts. We've normalized doing multiple things simultaneously not because we can't focus, but because focusing on **just one** thing feels like a waste of time. If I'm watching Netflix, I'll probably also be scrolling through my feed. If our mind is a web so we access few files at a time. It's not about distraction it's about maximizing time in a world that moves at breakneck speed.

Multitasking as a **Superpower** and a **Weakness**

Now, I won't pretend that multitasking doesn't come with its downsides. There's no denying that we, as Gen Z, tend to have shorter attention spans than previous generations. We expect everything to happen now. A loading screen longer than five seconds? Forget it I'm out. Video buffers for even a second? I'm already thinking of closing the tab and moving on "hatao bnch*d". We've been conditioned to crave instant gratification in every aspect of life, whether it's entertainment, information, or even social validation (thanks, Instagram likes).

But here's the thing: while this constant multitasking makes us faster and more efficient, it can also make us impatient. We don't have time for long, drawn-out explanations. It's like we have this internal clock ticking away in the back of our minds, reminding us that if something isn't immediately grabbing our attention, we've got 50 other things we could be doing instead. This impatience often gets mistaken for laziness, but it's not that. It's that we've learned how to optimize our time and attention in a world filled with endless distractions. Why spend 20 minutes reading a long-form article when a 60-second YouTube Short's can give me the same information?

This tendency to speed through life comes with trade-offs, though. Because we're always juggling, we might miss the details, the nuances, and the deeper thinking that some tasks require. Let's be real: we've all had that moment where we think we're listening to our professor on Zoom, but then we realize we've been completely zoned out for the last 10 minutes because we got too wrapped up in that text thread. I was listening to my Accounts teacher with full concentration and pen, then suddenly I went into my future office with the balance sheet in my hand that had everything in 100s crores and again I was back into class to catchup with the topic from my friends notebook . Fomo is real, and it manifests in how we interact with the world.

Spontaneity vs. **Overthinking**: The Gen Z Paradox

One of the most interesting contradictions within Gen Z's multitasking mindset is our ability to make decisions quickly but then spend hours, days, or even weeks overthinking those same decisions. We're spontaneous to the core. When we see something that looks cool, whether it's a new travel destination, a restaurant, or even a new trend we jump on it. There's no time to sit around and weigh the pros and cons because, in our world, if you don't act fast, you miss out.

But here's the kicker: once the decision is made, that's when the overthinking starts. Was it the right call? What if there was a better option? What if I miss out on something cooler? It's a constant cycle of **second-guessing**. We're fast decision-makers, sure, but we're also deep thinkers. It's just that we process our thoughts at lightning speed, and sometimes, that speed leads to doubt. This is one of the quirks that older generations don't understand about us. We can make decisions on the fly, but we also carry the weight of those decisions with us for a long time.

Take that trip I took last year, where we impulsively decided to ditch Goa and head to Manali. Sure, it was a fun trip, but I couldn't help but wonder if Goa would've been better, even while I was sitting there enjoying the view of the Mountains. That's the paradox of Gen Z: we move fast, but we also linger on the "what-ifs." We're adaptable, but that adaptability comes with its own set of anxieties.

Attention Spans: Is Shorter Always Worse?

Let's talk about this whole short attention span narrative. You've probably heard it a million times: Gen Z has the attention span of a goldfish, and we can't focus on anything for longer than a few seconds. While it's true that we're used to consuming bite-sized chunks of content, that doesn't mean we can't handle deep, complex ideas. It just means we've become experts at filtering out what's irrelevant. TRS 40 min podcast is consumed by Gen Z , how can you claim us not going into deep.

We've all been in that situation where we're scrolling through Instagram or TikTok, swiping past dozens of videos that don't grab our attention in the first two seconds. If a post doesn't hook us right away, it's out. But if something catches our eye whether it's a funny meme, a thought-provoking video, or an insightful comment—we're all in. We can go deep when it matters, but we've learned how to sift through the noise to get to what's important. It's not that we have short attention spans, it's that we've developed a kind of information **filter** that older generations don't understand.

And honestly, it's a survival skill in today's world. There's so much content out there that if we tried to give everything our full attention, we'd never get anything done. So, we prioritize. We focus on what matters most and leave the rest behind. In a sense, our shorter attention spans are actually an advantage. We don't waste time on the fluff. We get to the point and move on.

Technology Shaping Our **Minds**

Technology is the biggest driver of this multitasking mindset. Think about it: we've grown up with smartphones in our hands, and these devices are designed to help us do multiple things at once. We can text, email, watch videos, and browse social media all at the same time and we've gotten good at it. The tech we use daily is built to accommodate our need to switch between tasks rapidly, and that's reshaped the way we think.

Just look at the apps we use. Instagram has stories, posts, reels, DMs all in one place. TikTok is designed for endless scrolling, feeding us video after video with no breaks in between. Even our emails are sent in rapid-fire mode, and if someone doesn't respond within a few hours, we start wondering if they even saw it. Technology has made it so that we're constantly juggling tasks, and we've adapted accordingly.

Story about my brother trying to do an NEFT slow transfer while I was sitting there, transaction already completed via fast UPI? That's what I'm talking about. For us, speed is everything. If it's not fast, it's not worth our time. And this isn't just limited to social media or entertainment. It's how we handle everything from school assignments to social interactions. We expect things to happen quickly, and when they don't, we get frustrated.

Balancing Multitasking with **Mindfulness**

But here's where it gets tricky. While multitasking is a **superpower**, it's not always the best approach. There are times when we need to slow down, focus, and give something our full attention. We can't always be operating at high speed, switching between tasks without taking a moment to breathe. That's where mindfulness comes in. As much as we're wired for multitasking, there's also a growing awareness among Gen Z that we need to find moments of stillness, too.

You've probably noticed the rise of mindfulness apps like Calm or Headspace. More and more of us are recognizing that while multitasking is a trait but calmness is a key (even **Diljit Dosanjh** suggested to spend some time in calmness like yoga or praying)

FOUR

ATTACHED BUT DETACHED

Something most of us know all too well: social media. It's a world where most of Gen Z spends a big chunk of their time. It's a place where we connect, share, create, and consume. But there's more to it than meets the eye. Beneath the surface of endless scrolling, likes, and DMs, there's a duality to this experience—one that many of us feel but rarely talk about.

Social media has quickly become the heart of how we communicate, stay updated, and even form our identities. But with all its perks, it has this strange power. It's a force that can connect us while making us feel more isolated than ever before. What causes this paradox? Mark Zuckerberg's meta world. We're all in it together, yet somehow we're miles apart. Let's take a moment to reflect on this.

Social platforms are essentially a digital stage. Every day, millions of people put their best foot forward, showcasing moments of their lives whether it's a lavish meal, an exotic vacation, or just a casual Sunday hangout. But here's the thing: how much of this is genuine? And if it's not, why do we all play along?

There's a famous quote about social media that goes something like this: "If it's not on Instagram, did it even happen?" I think that sums it up perfectly. It's almost as if we're living through our screens, not fully engaged in the moments happening around us. This idea of living for the post is something we've all encountered at some point.

In our generation, it sometimes feels like if you're not posting, you're invisible. There's this unspoken pressure to put yourself out there, to document your life, and to curate it in a way that others will admire. And if you don't? Well, then you're not really "part of the conversation," are you?

But here's the part that confuses me the most: while we're all so focused on being connected, we're also becoming more de_tach_ed from each other, from our real selves, and from reality itself.

Think about it for a second. How many of us have two separate accounts on Instagram? There's the main account, which is polished, public, and very much designed for social approval. It's where we post the "good" parts of our lives, the ones that we want everyone to see, the ones that are safe for our families and employers to follow. But then there's the **"finsta"**, the private Instagram that only our closest friends follow ... pvtt. .... This is where the real stuff happens. It's where we post our rants, our frustrations, and our less-than-perfect moments. It's a more authentic space, but it's also a sign of the fragmentation we're experiencing in our social lives.

This divide between the main account and the finsta is symbolic of the split identity many of us are struggling with. We have to constantly decide what's worth sharing and what should be hidden. We're curating our lives in a way that almost feels like acting. And the more we do it, the more it feels like we're living two separate lives: the public one and the private one. How did we get here?

It's exhausting, isn't it? I know people who spend hours thinking about what to post, how to phrase their captions, and which filter to use. Everything is calculated, planned, and perfected. It's almost as if we're all playing this giant game of perception, where the goal is to get as many likes and followers as possible. But here's the question: are we really being ourselves? Or are we just playing a role?

I once read a study that said young people today feel more disconnected and lonely than ever before, despite being more "connected" through social media. Isn't that ironic? We have hundreds sometimes thousands of "friends" online, but how many of those people do we really know? How many of them can we turn to when things get tough? The reality is, social media friendships often lack the depth and authenticity of real-life connections.

This brings me to one of the most interesting dynamics I've noticed: the rise of online-only friendships. Let me give you an example. My PG roommate, let's call him rishuu - a thin boy with cunning eyes, is someone who's mastered the art of texting. He spends hours messaging girls on Instagram and WhatsApp, striking up conversations with people he's never met in person. On the surface, it looks like he's popular and well-connected. But here's the catch: he's never actually talked to any of these girls face-to-face.

In real life, Rishuu is shy, awkward, and unable to approach anyone. He'll see these girls on campus, but he'll never say a word. Why do you think that is?

It's almost like social media has given him a shield, a safe space where he can interact without the fear of rejection or judgment. But outside of that space, he's lost. And I think that's the case for a lot of us. We've become so comfortable behind our screens that we've forgotten how to engage with people in the real world.

This leads to another big issue: **trolling**. It's one of the darker sides of social media on Gen Z, and it's something that seems to be getting worse with time. Before the internet, if you had a problem with someone, you had to confront them face-to-face. But now? People can hide behind anonymous profiles and say the most horrible things, all without facing any real consequences.

You've probably seen it happen with celebrities. They'll post a picture, and within minutes, the comments section will be flooded with hate. People feel entitled to criticize their looks, their opinions, their choices. It's brutal, and it's not just happening to public figures. Have you ever been on the receiving end of online hate?

One of my favorite influencers took a break from social media recently because the trolling became unbearable. She was getting harassed every day, and it started to affect her mental health. It's a reminder that behind every profile, there's a real person with real feelings. But sometimes, it feels like we've forgotten that. Why do we allow this culture of online hate to thrive?

I think part of the problem is that we've started to blur the line between real life and the online world. We put so much value on what happens on social media that we start to lose sight of what really matters. I've seen this happen with some of my closest friends. One of them, let's call her Priya as she is uncomfortable to use her name is obsessed with documenting every moment of her life on Instagram. Whether it's a meal, a concert, or a casual coffee outing, she's always posting. But here's the thing: while she's busy trying to capture the perfect shot, she's missing out on the actual experience.

We went to a concert together once, and instead of dancing and enjoying the music, Priya spent the whole night filming it for her story. It was like she wasn't even there, more focused on her followers than on having a good time. Have you ever done something like that? Sacrificed the moment for the perfect post?

It's a trap so many of us fall into. We're so focused on how our lives look online that we forget to actually live them. And while we're chasing validation through likes and comments, we're missing out on the real-life connections that truly matter.

There's an interesting science behind this, too. Every time we get a like, the same chemical that makes us feel good when we eat our favorite food or win a game. Social media is literally addictive, and that's why we keep coming back for more. But here's the problem: it's never enough. No matter how many likes we get, we always want more.

I've seen people post something, then obsessively check their phones every few minutes to see how it's doing. If they don't get the response they were hoping for, it can completely ruin their mood. Does this sound familiar to you?

The Royal Society for Public Health did a study in 2019 and found that Instagram is the worst social media platform for young people's mental health. The constant pressure to be perfect, the endless comparison to others, and the fear of missing out (FOMO) are all taking a toll on us. And yet, we can't seem to stop.

In fact, even though I'm not as active on social media nowadays, as some of my friends, I've had moments where I've felt left out. I've seen pictures of my friends hanging out without me, and yeah, it stings. Social media has this weird way of making you feel connected and excluded at the same time.

What do you think about this?

-
-
-
-
-
-
-
-
-
-
-
-
-
-

There's a strange irony to the way social media has infiltrated our daily lives, one that I can't help but notice every single day. We wake up, check our phones, scroll through Instagram or Snapchat, and before we even get out of bed, we're already caught up in this digital world. What's even more bizarre is how often I catch myself doing something totally unrelated to social media, only to end up being sucked back into it. I'll pick up my phone to check the time or find a spelling for a word just something simple and quick and the next thing I know, I'm mindlessly scrolling through my feed, completely forgetting what I originally picked up my phone for.

I'm sure I'm not the only one who's experienced this. You start with something harmless, like looking up a recipe or responding to a text, and before you know it, you've lost 30 minutes watching videos on Instagram or snapping back and forth on Snapchat. It's almost like our phones have become traps, pulling us in every time we look at them. And while this might seem like a small, insignificant habit, it's actually a symptom of a much bigger problem, a kind of digital addiction that has become so normal for Gen Z that we don't even realize it's happening.

The way social media hooks us in is no accident. There's a reason why apps like Instagram, TikTok, and Snapchat are designed the way they are. They're built to keep us engaged, to make sure we're always coming back for more. Every notification, every like, every new follower triggers a tiny hit of dopamine in our brains. A physologist tech team constantly make change in platform so that it's same addictive as always. And the scary part is, it works.

This kind of mindless scrolling is something that has become so ingrained in our daily routines that we don't even question it anymore. We're constantly looking at our phones, refreshing our feeds, and checking for notifications, even when there's nothing new to see. And the worst part? It feels like we can't stop. We've become so dependent on our phones for entertainment, validation, and connection that the idea of going without them is even for a few hours, it feels impossiblllle.

But what's even more troubling is how social media is affecting our ability to focus and be present in the real world. Have you ever been out with friends, only to realize that everyone at the table is on their phones? You're supposed to be hanging out, talking, and enjoying each other's company, but instead, you're all scrolling through Instagram or sending snaps to other people. It's like we're together, but we're not really there. We're more connected to the people on our screens than we are to the people sitting right in front of us. And that, to me, is one of the most dangerous effects of social media. It's creating this strange detachment from the real world, where we're always **half-in**, **half-out**, never fully engaged with what's happening around us.

There's this pressure to constantly share what we're doing, where we are, and who we're with, like we need to prove to the world that we're living these exciting, fulfilled lives. But in reality, we're more focused on curating the perfect image for social media than we are on actually enjoying the moment. It's a weird, toxic cycle that's hard to break out of because the validation we get from likes, comments, and views feels so rewarding in the moment. But afterward, when the dopamine rush fades, we're left feeling empty, like something's missing.

It's not just about the time we waste on social media, either. It's about how it's changing the way we think, the way we interact with the world, and the way we view ourselves. Social media has created this culture of comparison, where we're constantly measuring ourselves against the people we see online. And let's be real most of the time, the people we're comparing ourselves to aren't even showing their real lives. They're showing the highlight reel, the best parts, the filtered, edited version of themselves that they want the world to see.

I know so many people who have fallen into this trap, myself included. We see these influencers or celebrities living these glamorous, picture-perfect lives, and we start to feel like we're not good enough. Like we're missing out. Like our own lives don't measure up. But the truth is, most of what we see on social media isn't real. It's a performance, a carefully crafted image designed to get likes and followers. And yet, we still fall for it. We still let it affect the way we feel about ourselves.

This constant comparison can take a serious toll on our mental health. Studies have shown that social media can lead to feelings of anxiety, depression, and low self-esteem, especially among young people. We're so focused on trying to live up to these unrealistic standards that we start to lose sight of what really matters our own happiness, our own experiences, our own sense of self-worth.

And it's not just about comparing ourselves to others, either. Social media has also changed the way we build relationships. I've seen it happen time and time again with my friends. They'll meet someone online, start talking, and before you know it, they're "friends." But here's the thing: they've never actually met in person. Their entire relationship exists behind a screen, through texts, snaps, and DMs. And while it might feel like a real connection, there's something missing. There's no face-to-face interaction, no real human connection. It's all just digital.

I've experienced this firsthand with one of my friends. He's been talking to this girl for months, texting her every day, sending snaps, liking her posts you know the drill. But here's the kick: he's never actually met her in person. They go to the same college, but whenever he sees her in real life, he freezes up. He can't talk to her face-to-face, even though they've been chatting online for months. It's like he's more comfortable behind a screen than he is in real life. And honestly, it's kind of sad. Social media has made it easier to connect with people, but it's also made those connections feel... less real. It's like we're losing the ability to talk to people face-to-face, to build real, meaningful relationships.

It's no wonder that so many people feel anxious and depressed after spending time on social media. We're constantly bombarded with images of other people's success, happiness, and beauty, and it can make us feel like we're not good enough. Like we're falling behind. But the truth is, none of it is real. Social media is a curated version of reality, one that's designed to make us feel like we need to keep up, like we need to be perfect.

So, what's the solution? How do we break free from this cycle of comparison and detachment? How do we find a balance between staying connected and staying grounded in reality? It's not easy, but I think it starts with being more mindful about how we use social media. We need

To reflect on how social media has woven itself into the very fabric of our everyday lives, it's clear that the challenges go beyond just mindless scrolling or the occasional distraction. Social media has fundamentally altered how we interact with the world, how we perceive our achievements, and how we view ourselves. It's a constant battle between being present in the moment and getting swept away by the allure of notifications, posts, and the desire to stay connected. However, despite all the negative effects, we can't ignore the positive aspects it brings. Like most things, it's all about balance.

One of the more subtle yet significant impacts of social media on Gen Z is how it shapes our sense of time. When we're constantly exposed to highlight reels of other people's lives, it creates this sense of urgency, as if we're falling behind if we're not achieving certain milestones at the same pace as everyone else. Social media makes us feel like everything needs to happen now. Graduating, landing a dream job, traveling to exotic places, finding a relationship these all become markers of success that we feel pressured to achieve as quickly as possible. If we see a peer doing something we haven't done yet, it's easy to start doubting ourselves.

This is a phenomenon is common. After scrolling through Instagram and seeing posts of friends graduating or working at well-known companies, I've found myself questioning whether I'm on the right track. Even though I know everyone has their own path, social media can make it feel like you're playing catch-up with everyone else's timeline. It's almost as if life becomes a race, where milestones are reduced to moments we can post about for validation.

This sense of urgency can also affect how we set goals. There's a constant desire to do more, achieve more, and showcase it all on social media. As a result, many of us in Gen Z struggle with burnout, trying to juggle too many responsibilities at once. We set unrealistic expectations for ourselves, fueled by what we see online, which only leads to stress and anxiety when things don't pan out the way we envisioned. We begin to measure our worth by external validation rather than internal satisfaction.

It's not just career or personal achievements that get caught in this race our social lives are affected too. There's a growing pressure to always be out and about, attending events, going on vacations, or having new experiences to document and share online. If you spend a weekend at home, it can feel like you're missing out on something, simply because your feed is full of people seemingly having the time of their lives.

But social media's influence extends even further, shaping the way we communicate and form relationships. In the age of Snapchat streaks and Instagram DMs, friendships often exist more in the digital realm than in real life. We send quick messages or exchange memes, but when was the last time we had a meaningful conversation without the filter of a screen? Social media encourages constant connection, but paradoxically, that connection is often shallow.

For example, I've noticed that my communication with friends often revolves around what's happening on social media. We'll send each other posts, react to stories, or talk about the latest trends. While it keeps us in touch, it sometimes feels like we're not really connecting on a **deeper** level. It's easy to mistake these digital interactions for real, meaningful engagement, but the truth is, nothing can replace the value of face-to-face conversations or shared experiences in real life.

I've seen relationships evolve or sometimes deteriorate because of social media's role in how we interact. Arguments can start over a missed text or an ignored snap, and jealousy can creep in when we see our friends hanging out with others without us. Social media can create a false sense of competition in our friendships, where we feel like we're constantly trying to maintain our place in someone's life based on how much we interact with them online. This creates an unhealthy dynamic that didn't exist before, where relationships are measured by digital exchanges rather than real emotional connection.

Even romantic relationships have been impacted by social media in ways that can be both positive and negative. On the one hand, apps like Snapchat and Instagram make it easy to stay in touch with someone, to share moments throughout the day, and to feel closer even when physically apart. On the other hand, these same platforms can introduce insecurities, especially when we're constantly exposed to others' idealized relationships or when communication becomes more about maintaining a public image than genuinely connecting with a partner.

People have experienced anxiety about their relationships simply because their significant other didn't post about them or respond to their stories quickly enough. Social media creates this expectation that if someone isn't showing you off online, they must not care as much. It's a toxic mindset that can erode trust and communication in a relationship. We've started equating online visibility with real-world affection, which is a dangerous line to walk.

This brings me back to the core issue: the addictive nature of social media and how it's designed to keep us coming back. The instant gratification we get from likes, comments, and shares is short-lived but incredibly powerful. It's why we often find ourselves reaching for our phones even when we don't have a specific reason to. Just like how I'll sometimes pick up my phone to look up a spelling and then end up on Instagram, this habitual checking becomes second nature. It's as if our brains have been rewired to seek that constant validation from the digital world.

The algorithms behind these platforms are tailored to our behavior, feeding us content that keeps us engaged for longer periods of time. Whether it's a funny video, a shocking news story, or a friend's latest post, the content is always evolving, always enticing. It's this endless stream of stimulation that keeps us hooked, and it's no surprise that it can be so hard to put our phones down once we've started scrolling.

And yet, for all the negative aspects of social media, I can't deny that it has its advantages. It's a tool that has revolutionized the way we communicate, share ideas, and stay informed. Platforms like Instagram, Twitter, and TikTok have given rise to social movements, allowed marginalized voices to be heard, and enabled people to build communities around shared interests. I see how social media can bring people together for a common cause or help someone find their tribe (eg. All eyes on Rafah , black lives matter)

In my involvement with the Robin Hood Army (RHA), social media played a huge role in organizing drives, spreading awareness, and recruiting volunteers. We were able to connect with like-minded individuals who wanted to make a difference in the community, and it was all thanks to the reach and power of social media. It's a reminder that while these platforms can be distracting, they also have the potential to create real, meaningful change when used with purpose.

The key, I think, lies in being more mindful about how we use social media. It's about recognizing when we're falling into the trap of mindless scrolling or seeking validation and making a conscious effort to step back. It's not about quitting social media entirely.... it's about finding a balance between the digital world and the real one. We need to set boundaries for ourselves, whether it's limiting screen time, turning off notifications, or making time for offline activities that bring us joy.

One strategy I've found helpful is scheduling specific times to check social media, rather than constantly dipping in and out throughout the day. This helps me stay focused on what I'm doing without the temptation to get sidetracked by my phone. I've also started being more intentional about who I follow and what kind of content I consume. By curating my feed to include only the things that inspire or educate me, I've reduced the amount of time I spend mindlessly scrolling through content that doesn't add value to my life.

It's also important to remember that not everything needs to be shared online. Sometimes, the best moments are the ones we keep to ourselves or share with the people we're with in real life. By stepping away from the need to document everything for social media, we can start to reclaim our experiences and be more present in the moment.

In the end, social media is a tool, a powerful one that can either enhance our lives or take away from them, depending on how we choose to use it. It's up to us to decide whether we want to be controlled by it or take control of our relationship with it. As Gen Z, we're the first generation to grow up fully immersed in the digital age, and that comes with both challenges and opportunities. But if we can learn to navigate this landscape with intention and awareness, we can strike a balance between being connected and staying grounded.

It's a journey I'm still figuring out for myself, but one thing is clear: social media isn't going away anytime soon. It's up to us to create a healthier, more mindful relationship with it one where we can enjoy the benefits without losing ourselves in the process.

FIVE

DIY LEARNERS

Let's dive into one of the most exciting things about being a part of Gen Z..... the way we learn. The world has changed so much in the past couple of decades, and education is no exception. While previous generations had to follow a strict, traditional path of school, college, degrees—our generation has taken learning into our own hands. We have the internet, and that means we have endless access to information, skills, and new knowledge. For Gen Z, the digital world isn't just a place to hang out or post selfies. It's our classroom, our teacher, our resource for becoming the best versions of ourselves.

I still remember the first time I got hooked on beatboxing. It was completely by accident. I was watching America's Got Talent, and there was this guy named Neil Alam who blew my mind. He was creating entire musical beats just with his mouth. I'd never seen anything like it, and it was one of those moments where I knew I had to learn how to do that. So what did I do? I didn't sign up for any classes or get a tutor, nope! Instead, I went straight to YouTube and started watching videos. That's where I found tutorials, breakdowns, and even live sessions from beatboxers all around the world. Within a year, I was doing pretty solid beats myself. And here's the best part... it didn't cost me a rupee.

Now, imagine explaining that to someone from a previous generation. "Oh, I learned how to beatbox from YouTube." They'd probably think I was crazy, like how could anyone **really** learn something like that without going through traditional lessons, YouTube is just for entertainment? But that's the thing with Gen Z—we don't have to follow the same path. We've got the world at our fingertips, literally, and we know how to make the most of it. Another example that hits home for me is digital marketing. I came across an ad on Instagram for a webinar on digital marketing, and I was curious. I'd heard that digital marketing was the next big thing, so I thought, why not give it a shot? I signed up, attended the webinar, and from there, I took an online course. Fast forward a bit, and I was learning all the skills I needed to become proficient in digital marketing, a skill that would have taken years in a traditional setting.

And it's not just me. So many of us Gen Zers have realized that the internet is the perfect place to pick up new skills and even build careers. The digital ecosystem is our playground, just like the real fields were for millennials or even older generations. Sure, urbanization has taken away a lot of those open spaces where kids used to play, but we've found a new space online. It's where we learn, grow, and thrive. The convenience, the speed, and the accessibility of online learning fit perfectly with our fast-paced lives. We don't have the time or patience to sit in classrooms for years before we can start applying what we've learned. We want to dive right in, experiment, and make things happen. That's why platforms like YouTube, Coursera, ChatGPT, Udemy, and Wiseup have become so important to us.

This shift toward online learning and self-teaching is one of the defining characteristics of our generation. Gen Z has developed a "DIY learning" mindset. We're curious, and we want answers fast. Whether it's learning how to code, how to start a business, or even how to cook, we can find step-by-step guides, instructional videos, and online communities ready to help. We've grown up with Google as our go-to for everything. If we don't know how to do something, we'll search for it and have the answer in seconds. It's made us more independent learners and problem-solvers. And we don't wait for someone to teach us; we take charge of our own learning process.

For Gen Z, the internet isn't just a place to consume content—it's a resource for self-improvement.Think about how often you've Googled something in the past week. How many times have you watched a YouTube video to figure something out, whether it's how to change a tire, edit a video, or understand a complicated math problem? The information is out there, and we know how to find it. That's what sets us apart from older generations.

The traditional education system... schools, colleges, degrees still exists, but for Gen Z, it's not the only path. Many of us are starting to question whether we even need to go through the traditional system to succeed. Why spend years in college getting a degree when we can learn the same thing online, often faster and for a fraction of the cost? Yes, but primary schooling is important for discipline and curriculum. In fact, a survey conducted by Pearson found that nearly 60% of Gen Z believe that non-traditional pathways to education, like online courses, are just as valuable as a college degree. And that's because we've seen it work. We've seen people build successful careers without ever setting foot in a college classroom. The internet has leveled the playing field, giving us the tools we need to compete in the job market without necessarily following the same steps as our parents or older siblings. Curiosity is one of the driving forces behind this DIY learning mindset. Gen Z has grown up in a world where information is everywhere, and our curiosity pushes us to explore that information. We're not content to just accept things at face value but we want to dig deeper, understand more, and figure things out for ourselves.

In the past, if you had a question, you'd have to wait until you could ask a teacher or find a book on the topic. Now, we can satisfy our curiosity instantly. Want to know how a black hole works? There's a TED Talk for that. Want to learn how to play the guitar? There are thousands of tutorials online. The speed at which we can access information feeds our curiosity and drives us to keep learning.

One of the coolest things about being a part of Gen Z is that learning doesn't stop at school. We learn all the time, in every aspect of our lives. Whether we're scrolling through TikTok or watching a documentary on Netflix, we're picking up new information and skills. And the best part? We can apply what we learn almost immediately.

Let's go back to my beatboxing journey for a second. After watching those YouTube tutorials, I didn't just sit back and wait for more lessons. I practiced. I tried out new beats, experimented with sounds, and figured out what worked for me. The same thing happened with digital marketing. After taking that course, I didn't wait to get a job in the field—I started applying what I learned right away, testing out strategies, and seeing results. That's the beauty of online learning. It's not just about consuming information—it's about doing. We're hands-on learners, and the internet gives us the freedom to learn by doing. One of the things that makes online learning so unique is the social aspect of it. Learning isn't just a solitary activity anymore. There are entire communities online dedicated to sharing knowledge and helping others learn. Whether it's Reddit threads, Discord groups, or Instagram pages, Gen Z has built a culture of collaboration when it comes to learning.

I can't even count how many times I've joined an online forum or community to ask questions, share ideas, or get feedback. It's like having a classroom full of experts, ready to help you whenever you need it. And the best part? These communities are global. We're not limited by geography. We can learn from people all over the world, gaining new perspectives and insights that we wouldn't have access to in a traditional classroom setting. Of course, there are challenges that come with DIY learning. One of the biggest ones is staying motivated. When you're learning on your own, there's no teacher or deadline pushing you to keep going. It's easy to get distracted or give up when things get tough. Another challenge is the sheer amount of information available. With so many resources out there, it can be overwhelming to know where to start or which information to trust. Not all online courses are created equal, and not all information is accurate. It takes a certain level of critical thinking to navigate the digital learning landscape and find the best resources.

But even with these challenges, Gen Z has proven time and time again that we're capable of overcoming them. We're resourceful, determined, and willing to put in the work to achieve our goals. So, what does all this mean for the future of education? As Gen Z continues to push the boundaries of traditional learning, we're likely to see more and more people turning to online platforms for their education. Colleges and universities are already starting to adapt, offering online courses and degree programs to meet the needs of a generation that values flexibility and independence.But it's not just about formal education. Lifelong learning is becoming the norm. As technology continues to evolve, so too will the ways we learn. The internet has given us the tools to keep learning, growing, and adapting, no matter where we are in life.

So now I want to ask you, the reader: What's your story? How have you used the internet to learn something new? Have you taken an online course, taught yourself a new skill, or joined an online community? What do you think

SIX
INSTANT GRATIFICATION

Today wasn't exactly my best day, so I'm sitting here writing this with a pretty low mood. It's been hectic from start to finish, and I ended up in an argument with one of my friends.

Let me tell you how my day went. We had our university elections today, and as an active member of the ABVP party, I had to be present throughout. It was a crazy day because, for the first time, so many students came out to vote for both the college and DUSU elections. I think we did a good job campaigning, but man, it was exhausting. After the whole election madness, I had to rush back to my room because I had my IELTS tuition. Yep, I'm taking the IELTS since I plan to go abroad for my master's, but we'll get into that later.

Anyway, the metro ride home was another low point of my day. As usual, being a young guy, I didn't get a seat—typical Delhi Metro stuff. There was one seat left, but of course, it was reserved for ladies, and I wasn't going to take that. My phone battery decided to die on me, and to top it off, I didn't have enough cash to grab something to eat, which I usually do—just ₹15 for the battery auto ride from the metro to my room. When I finally got back home, my tiffin only had yellow dal and a sabji I wouldn't touch even on a good day. I forced myself to eat a little, hoping I'd treat myself to some chicken biryani later. Completely drained, I crashed on my bed and plugged in my phone to charge. Just as I was about to drift off, I got a message from my friend who'd been calling me for hours. He wanted me to pick up some clothes he'd left at my place since he was going home for the weekend. I wasn't in the mood, so I snapped and cut the call.

After waking up and finally having my biryani, I checked my phone and saw a dozen missed calls from home, friends, and, of course, those annoying study-abroad counseling agencies that love to spam. So yeah, it was one of those days. But here I am, writing the book I've promised myself I'd finish. Speaking of which, let me share the plan I've got for this book. I've framed the structure, outlined the chapters, and written bits and pieces for each. Now, I'm focusing on fleshing it out. I hope it turns out well, even though today wasn't my day.

As the day was pretty fast elections, classes and arguments this brings me to the point digital natives: **The Need for Speed**

As Gen Z, we're born into a world where everything happens fast—information, entertainment, news, you name it. We've got all the tools we need to get whatever we want at the tip of a finger. And because we've always had this access, we expect everything else in life to work the same way. But let me tell you, this doesn't always work out in our favor. For example, in the metro today, I couldn't check anything on my phone since it died, and I realized how much I rely on it to stay connected, entertained, and informed. It got me thinking about how we're so used to instant answers that even the slightest delay feels unbearable.

Our entire generation has grown up with smartphones, tablets, and computers. We are true digital natives, and while this has its perks, it also comes with some challenges. We're constantly bombarded with information, and sometimes it feels overwhelming. We're used to swiping through things so fast that we don't always take time to slow down and process what's important. That's one reason why our attention span is so short. I mean, when was the last time any of us watched a 10-minute video without checking the time halfway through? It's no wonder short-form content like Instagram Reels and TikTok have taken off.

Binge-Watching Culture

Then there's the binge-watching thing. Man, do we love to binge-watch. Gone are the days when people had to wait a whole week for the next episode of a TV show. Now, we can watch an entire season in one sitting. But here's the thing—while it's great to have this option, it also spoils us a bit. We get so used to instant entertainment that the idea of waiting for anything becomes frustrating.

I've seen friends finish entire series over the weekend. Even I'm guilty of it—once, during a long weekend, I watched back-to-back seasons of a show on Netflix. The result? I was so consumed by the show that I felt this weird sense of emptiness when it ended. That's the thing with binge-watching: it's fun in the moment, but it also feeds into this craving for instant gratification. We want more, and we want it now. The whole process of waiting for things to happen doesn't sit well with us anymore. Why wait when you can have it all now, right? But that comes at a cost. When we get everything immediately, we lose patience with things that take time—things like studying for exams, working toward career goals, or even relationships. We've been conditioned to expect everything on demand, but life doesn't always work that way. Sometimes, we have to wait, work hard, and be patient—things that don't come naturally to our fast-paced, digital-first generation.

Fast Results in Education: The Pressure Cooker

Speaking of impatience, let's talk about education. As a Gen Z, I've noticed that we tend to want quick wins in everything we do. We want to ace our exams, get top jobs, and learn new skills—fast. The traditional education system doesn't always fit with our mindset. It's slow, methodical, and requires long-term commitment. But in a world where you can learn how to code or master a skill on YouTube in just a few hours, sitting through a semester-long course can feel like a drag.

Take my IELTS tuition, for example. I know it's important, and I need it for my master's, but every class feels like it's going on forever. My mind keeps drifting, thinking about the things I could be doing instead—working on my social media strategy, learning a new beatboxing trick, or even just catching up on the latest Netflix series. This is the reality for many of us. We're juggling so many things at once that we expect everything to move at lightning speed. We're the multitasking generation. Pressure Cooker has so much pressure inside and with the help of this it makes the food ready, same with us. Sometimes, our need for fast results comes at the cost of depth. We might learn a lot of things quickly, but how much of it really sticks? The digital ecosystem has allowed us to access knowledge at our fingertips, but the challenge is to stay focused long enough to really absorb it.

Impact on Long-Term Goals: The Clash

And that brings me to the biggest challenge we face as a generation: balancing our need for instant gratification with our long-term goals. We're so used to getting things fast—whether it's food delivery, likes on Instagram, or answers from Google that we struggle with things that require time, effort, and patience. This can be a real problem when it comes to pursuing long-term goals like education, career growth, or even personal development.

I've seen so many of my friends get frustrated when they don't see immediate results. They'll start something like a new hobby, a side hustle, or even a relationship and if it doesn't pay off right away, they move on. I've been guilty of this too. There have been times when I started learning something new, only to give up because it wasn't clicking fast enough. The idea of sticking with something for the long haul seems daunting when we're so used to quick wins. But here's the thing, some of the best things in life take time. Building a career, mastering a skill, or even just growing as a person takes patience. And while it's hard for us to wrap our heads around that concept, it's something we need to learn if we want to succeed in the long run.

This is just the first part of the chapter. As we continue, I'll dive deeper into how we can balance our desire for instant gratification with the reality that some things in life just take time. But for now, I hope this gives you a glimpse into how Gen Z's need for speed shapes everything from our education to our entertainment choices.

As I sit here, still digesting today's craziness, one thing keeps running through my head—how impulsive I've been lately. Snapping at my friend, almost missing my IELTS class because I just couldn't focus after the elections, or even thinking about ordering biryani before I even checked my bank balance. It all feels so in-the-moment, but that's kind of what this chapter is all about—how we, as Gen Z, often act on impulse because of our need for instant gratification. And it's a struggle, believe me.

Impulsivity vs. Planning: The Clash

We've been raised in a time when everything is right at our fingertips. Need a ride? Open an app and a cab's at your door in minutes. Want food? Just scroll through Zomato and it's there, hot and fresh. It's no surprise that this constant availability makes us a little impulsive. Why wait when you can have it now, right? I'm sure you've experienced it too. I mean, how many times have you planned to save up for something big, only to blow it on a sale because, well, the offer was just too good to resist? This mindset is great for short-term wins but, honestly, it's a killer when it comes to long-term planning. Take my IELTS prep, for instance. It's not something you can cram for in a few days or swipe through like Instagram stories. It requires discipline, focus, and most importantly, planning (specially for a person like me, who makes so much spelling mistakes) . That's where Gen Z faces the real challenge—sticking to something when the results aren't immediate.

Unlike previous generations, who were used to slow progress and working toward goals over long periods, we're used to things happening fast. Our parents planned their lives in a way that allowed for steady growth. They didn't have the luxury of clicking a button and having food, clothes, or entertainment delivered instantly. Instead, they saved up, they waited, they built things over time. For them, planning wasn't just important—it was essential for survival.

But us? We're different. We're used to a world that moves at warp speed. As a result, planning feels tedious, almost unnecessary at times. Why plan out your day when you can just wing it and get things done on the go? But here's the catch—life doesn't always work that way. Long-term success, whether in our careers, relationships, or personal growth, requires careful planning. And that's something many of us struggle with because it feels like the opposite of everything we've grown up with. I'm not going to lie—this whole need for speed messes with our heads. On days like today, where everything feels like it's moving a mile a minute, it's hard not to feel overwhelmed. And I'm not alone in this. As a generation, we're under a lot of pressure to keep up with the fast pace of life. We want everything now success, happiness, validation and when it doesn't come instantly, it takes a toll on our mental health.

Look at social media, for example. We post something, and within seconds, we're checking for likes, comments, and shares. It's like a drug, and the high doesn't last long. If the likes don't roll in fast enough, we start questioning ourselves—Was the post not good enough? Am I not interesting enough? This constant need for instant feedback is exhausting. It puts us in a loop of seeking validation from others instead of focusing on our own growth.

Compare this to our parents or even millennials. They weren't raised with this kind of immediate feedback loop. Sure, they had challenges of their own, but they didn't grow up with the same constant pressure to perform and be validated online. They had time to figure things out, to grow at their own pace. We, on the other hand, feel like we're in a race, constantly trying to keep up with everyone else.

The impact on our mental health is undeniable. Anxiety, depression, burnout—it's all too common among Gen Z. We're a generation that's constantly "on," always connected, always looking for the next thing. The worst part is, we're often too busy chasing the next hit of instant gratification to realize that we're burning out in the process. I remember during one particularly tough week, I had exams, project deadlines, and some social commitments that I had to juggle. I was so caught up in trying to do everything at once that I barely slept, barely ate, and by the end of it, I felt completely drained. And for what? A few quick wins that didn't even last. It's moments like these that make me realize how much our generation sacrifices our well-being for the sake of immediacy.

The Future of Instant Gratification: Where Are We Headed?

So, where does this all lead? Are we doomed to be forever stuck in this cycle of instant gratification, or is there hope for us yet? Honestly, I think it's a bit of both.

On the one hand, technology isn't slowing down anytime soon. If anything, it's only going to get faster. We're already seeing AI tools that can generate art, write essays, and even predict our shopping preferences before we've made a decision. The future is all about speed, and as a generation that thrives on fast results, we're perfectly positioned to take advantage of that. But there's a downside to this as well. As things continue to speed up, our patience will only wear thinner, and our ability to focus on long-term goals will be tested more than ever before.

On the flip side, I think Gen Z is also starting to realize the drawbacks of this fast-paced lifestyle. We're more aware of mental health than any generation before us, and that's a good thing. We know that living life at full speed all the time isn't sustainable, and many of us are actively seeking ways to slow down, to practice mindfulness, and to find a balance between instant gratification and long-term fulfillment.

So, how do we balance our need for speed with the reality that some things just take time? Here are a few things I've learned along the way—some from personal experience, and some from watching others navigate this crazy digital age we live in:

1. **Set Small Goals for Big Wins** : It's easy to get discouraged when your big goals feel too far away. Break them down into smaller, more manageable tasks that give you quick wins along the way. This helps feed your need for instant results while still keeping you on track for the bigger picture. Like take my eg. Firstly, I started

working on a research paper on Gen Z and as soon it was completed my way for this book was clear.

2. **Practice Patience** : This sounds cliché, but it's true. Not everything in life can be delivered with the speed of Amazon Prime. Whether it's building a career, mastering a skill, or developing a meaningful relationship, some things just take time. Learn to be okay with that.

3. **Limit Your Screen Time** : I know, easier said than done. But seriously, try it. Take breaks from your phone, especially social media. It's amazing how much better you'll feel when you're not constantly glued to a screen. I reduced my reels consumption and now it feels better in term of focus.

4. **Focus on Depth, Not Speed** : Whether you're learning something new or working on a project, try to focus on doing it well, rather than doing it fast. It's tempting to rush through things just to get them done, but quality often suffers when we're in too much of a hurry.

5. **Celebrate Progress, Not Just Results** : One thing I've learned is that progress itself is something to be celebrated. You don't always need to wait for the end result to feel good about yourself. Celebrate the small steps along the way—it makes the journey more enjoyable.
As Arijit Singh sang " safar Khubsoorat hain manzil se bhi "

And so, as I reflect on today's events—the hectic election day, the rushed metro ride, the impulsive decisions—I realize that this is what it means to live as a Gen Z in the digital age. We're constantly pulled between the need for speed and the reality that some things just take time. It's not always easy, but it's the world we've been handed.

So, to my fellow Gen Z readers: How do you cope with this fast-paced life? Do you find yourself acting impulsively, or are you a planner at heart? Have you managed to find balance in a world that moves at lightning speed. We all must have.

SEVEN
PURPOSE & SUCCESS

As you might already know, I'm planning to go abroad for my studies next year. But getting there isn't as simple as packing a suitcase and hopping on a flight. To make it happen, I've been working like crazy to enhance my profile. Over the past few months, I've written two research papers, participated in NGO campaigns, and even kickstarted my beatboxing hobby again. It's been a whirlwind, juggling college, society work, and personal projects. And if that wasn't enough, my friends keep suggesting that I dive into the stock market. Yeah, you heard that right—the stock market! Just five years ago, stocks were something uncles talked about over chai, but now, even college students are knee-deep in it. It's crazy how much has changed.

Conversations with my friends aren't about what Netflix series to binge only anymore. Nope, they're about which new IPO is coming up, how many slots you're applying for, and which industry to bet on. Gen Z is all about the stock market and making money. I have a classmate who started modeling in his first year, and others who are raking in cash through reels and content creation. Five years ago, if you were a millennial, your final year in college was all about internships and applying for jobs. But today, Gen Z doesn't want to wait around for someone to hand them a paycheck—they want to create their own streams of income. And it's not just about making money, either. Gen Z is ambitious. Take my friend Manjot, for instance. He's got his eyes set on owning a Rolls Royce one day. Now, think about that for a second. A luxury car that costs more than most people's houses—and he's got a plan for how he's going to make that happen. He's not waiting for someone to tell him what's realistic; he's setting his own goals and figuring out how to achieve them. That's the mindset Gen Z brings to the table—big dreams, and the belief that they can make those dreams a reality.

Redefining Success: From Stability to Flexibility

For us, success isn't defined the same way it was for previous generations. Our parents, and even millennials, saw success as climbing the corporate ladder, landing a stable job, and maybe buying a house. But Gen Z? We value flexibility over stability. We don't want to be tied down to a 9-to-5 job unless it aligns with our passions and allows us to make an impact. A lot of my friends are working multiple jobs freelancing, starting their own side businesses, creating content—and they love it. It's not that we don't want to work hard, it's just that we want the freedom to choose how we work and what we work on.

Take my own experience, for example. Look at the whole marketing in your business is a huge responsibility, especially when you're balancing it with college, personal growth, and everything else. My hotel business back in Patna requires a lot of attention, especially as we're always looking for new ways to stay competitive and improve our customer experience. But at the same time, I'm deeply involved in university politics, trying to make a difference within the student community. It's tough to juggle both, but I do it because I believe success isn't just about making money, it's about making an impact. That's what drives me.

Gen Z is all about finding a balance between professional success and personal fulfillment. We're not content with the idea of working 40 years at a job just to retire. Instead, we want to work on things that matter to us, things that align with our values and passions. I've always been passionate about sustainable development and improving the business landscape in Patna, for example. So, I try to incorporate those values into the work I do at my hotels. It's not just about turning a profit..... it's about creating something meaningful and sustainable.

Social Causes: **Making an Impact While Making Money**

One of the most remarkable things about Gen Z is our commitment to social causes. Whether it's climate change, gender equality, or mental health awareness, we're not just sitting on the sidelines—we're actively getting involved. I and lot of my friends are deeply engaged in NGO work or using their platforms to raise awareness about important issues, like Fatima a Gen Z girl with her Humraahi Foundation . And for us, these social causes are not just hobbies or extracurricular activities. They're integral to **our definition of success.**

In my case, participating in NGO campaigns has been one of the most fulfilling things I've done. I remember one particular campaign where we focused on educating underprivileged children in Central Delhi. It was exhausting work—hot days, long hours, and limited resources—but the sense of purpose I felt was indescribable. I realized then that making an impact isn't just something you do on the side; it's something that can be woven into every aspect of your life, including your career. For Gen Z, the lines between work, social responsibility, and personal fulfillment are blurred. We don't see them as separate entities. Instead, we want to integrate them into a cohesive whole. That's why you'll find a lot of Gen Z entrepreneurs who are as committed to solving social problems as they are to growing their businesses. Whether it's ethical fashion brands, eco-friendly startups, or mental health apps, Gen Z is focused on using business as a tool for change.

And let's not forget our involvement in politics. As a member of the ABVP a student union , I've seen firsthand how passionate Gen Z is about making a difference in the world. We're not just waiting for change to happen; we're actively trying to create it. And the best part is, we're doing it in our own way—through social media campaigns, grassroots movements, and even by running for student office.

Comparison with Previous Generations: Breaking the Mold

If you look at the way previous generations approached life, there's a clear difference. For them, success was often measured by stability—getting a secure job, buying a house, and settling down. That was the dream. But for Gen Z, **stability isn't the end goal—it's flexibility, purpose, and impact**. We don't want to be confined by the traditional rules of success. Instead, we're carving out our own paths.

Millennials, for example, came of age during the rise of the internet and social media, and they embraced these new tools to build their careers. But Gen Z? We've grown up with these technologies. We're digital natives. We don't just use technology—we live and breathe it. And that changes everything. For us, success isn't about climbing the corporate ladder—it's about using the tools at our disposal to create something new, something that reflects who we are and what we care about.

In fact, a lot of the traditional milestones of success—like owning a home or working for a big company—just don't resonate with us. We'd rather rent than buy, freelance than commit to one employer, and start our own businesses rather than work for someone else. This mindset shift is huge, and it's transforming the way we think about work, life, and the future. Take my friend Manjot's Rolls Royce dream, for example. Ten or twenty years ago, that would have been seen as unrealistic, maybe even reckless. But today, with the rise of online businesses, freelancing, and content creation, it's entirely possible. Gen Z doesn't just dream big—we believe those dreams can come true if we're willing to work for anything. As Gen Z, we've entered adulthood with a totally different perspective on what it means to be successful. And while some of us might still follow traditional paths, like getting degrees and working our way up the career ladder, we're redefining success by blending ambition with purpose and passion. In the second half of this chapter, I want to dig deeper into how Gen Z's approach to career paths, financial independence, and social impact is different from previous generations, and how we are shaping the future with this mindset.

For many Gen Z individuals, financial independence is about much more than just earning a paycheck—it's about having the freedom to do what we want, when we want. We don't just dream about financial security; we want financial independence as soon as possible, and we're actively working toward it in ways that might have seemed unconventional just a decade ago. A lot of my friends are already making money through non-traditional channels. Whether it's through content creation on platforms like Instagram and TikTok, freelancing, or investing in the stock market, Gen Z has figured out that there are many ways to earn an income besides the typical 9-to-5 job. One of my closest friends started dabbling in the stock market during our second year of college, and now he's practically a day trader. It's funny to think that just a few years ago, most people would've said stock markets were the domain of older, more experienced investors. But now, young people are diving in headfirst, educating themselves through YouTube, blogs, and forums.

We've also embraced the gig economy. If you scroll through platforms like Fiverr, Upwork, or even Instagram, you'll find countless Gen Zers offering services ranging from graphic design to digital marketing to tutoring. It's become a new way for us to earn money on our own terms, outside the confines of a traditional corporate job.

In fact, I was recently chatting with some of my classmates, and the topic of side hustles came up. Nearly everyone in the group had some sort of side gig—from selling art prints online to tutoring high school students, to flipping sneakers for profit. And it's not just about making a few extra bucks; it's about developing a sense of control over our own financial destinies. We're not waiting around for someone to hand us an opportunity—we're creating our own.

Flexibility over Stability: The New Career Path

Another big shift in the way Gen Z views success is our focus on flexibility rather than stability. For older generations, success was often tied to long-term stability and getting a secure job with benefits, working there for decades, and then retiring comfortably. But for us, stability doesn't have the same appeal. In fact, many Gen Zers see it as restrictive. We crave flexibility. We want the ability to work from anywhere, to pursue our passions, and to switch career paths when something new and exciting comes along. The idea of staying in one job or one industry for our entire career feels outdated to many of us. Instead, we're more likely to pursue multiple career paths over the course of our lives. And thanks to the rise of remote work and the digital economy, that's more possible now than ever before.

Take my own life as an example. I've been involved in business, I've explored digital marketing, and I'm passionate about sustainability. I know that in the future, I'll probably move between industries or even combine my interests in ways that might not seem traditional, as I like manufacturing. And that's the beauty of being Gen Z. We have the tools, the knowledge, and the confidence to create careers that work for us, rather than fitting into predefined molds.

But this flexibility comes with its own challenges. The constant change can be stressful, and the pressure to always be hustling, to always be **"on,"** can take a toll on mental health. For many Gen Zers, the fear of missing out or falling behind pushes us to take on more than we can handle. Balancing multiple jobs or side gigs, while also maintaining a social life and personal well-being, is tough. We're still figuring out how to manage it all, but I think we're getting there.

Purpose and Impact: A New Definition of Success

For Gen Z, success isn't just about personal achievements it's about making a difference. We want to leave a positive mark on the world, whether that's through social causes, environmental sustainability, or advocating for mental health. It's not enough to just climb the ladder; we want to know that the ladder we're climbing is leading somewhere meaningful.

This is something I've thought about a lot in my own life. Being involved in university politics has shown me how important it is to use our voices for change. Whether it's advocating for student rights or pushing for more environmentally conscious policies, I've realized that success, for me, isn't just about growing my business or building my personal brand, it's also about contributing to something bigger than myself. And I'm not alone in feeling this way. So many of my peers are passionate about making a difference, whether it's fighting climate change, promoting equality, or supporting mental health initiatives. We want our work to have purpose, and we're willing to take risks and challenge the status quo to make that happen.

One example is the rise of purpose-driven businesses. Many Gen Z entrepreneurs are starting companies that are focused not just on profit, but on solving social and environmental problems. Whether it's ethical fashion brands that focus on sustainable materials, or tech startups that provide mental health resources, our generation is finding ways to combine purpose with profit.

When you compare Gen Z's approach to success with that of previous generations, the differences are clear. For Baby Boomers and Gen Xers, success was often about security—owning a home, having a stable job, and building a retirement fund. Millennials, too, pursued similar goals, though they were more focused on work-life balance and finding jobs that aligned with their personal values. I totally agree that was accordingly to the post **LPG** era (Libralization , privatization and Globlaztion) where people had to build their basics, but now it's totally different.

But for Gen Z, the priorities have shifted. We're more focused on flexibility, purpose, and making an impact. We're not as interested in owning homes or working at the same job for decades. Instead, we value experiences over possessions, and we're willing to take risks to pursue our passions and make a difference in the world. In some ways, this shift reflects the times we're living in. We've grown up in a world that's constantly changing, with new technologies, social movements, and global challenges emerging all the time. As a result, we're more adaptable, more willing to take risks, and more open to non-traditional paths to success.

But it also means that we face unique challenges. The pressure to always be **"on,"** to constantly hustle, and to make an impact can be overwhelming. And while the pursuit of flexibility and purpose is exciting, it can also be stressful—especially when you're trying to figure out how to pay the bills at the same time.

Practical Tips for Navigating the Gen Z Mindset

So, what does all of this mean for Gen Z as we move forward? How can we balance our ambitions with the realities of life? Here are a few practical tips that I've learned along the way:

1. **Prioritize Self-Care** : It's easy to get caught up in the hustle, but taking care of your mental and physical health is crucial. Whether it's setting boundaries with work, practicing mindfulness, or just taking time to relax, self-care should be a priority.

2. **Embrace Failure** : Not everything is going to work out perfectly, and that's okay. Gen Z is a generation of risk-takers, but with risk comes failure. Learn from your mistakes and keep moving forward. Personally I don't embrace failure, but still try to digest it.

3. **Stay Flexible** : The world is changing fast, and so are our opportunities. Stay open to new possibilities and be willing to pivot when necessary. Success doesn't have to follow a straight line, follow curves, it feels amazing.

4. **Find Your Purpose** : Whether it's through your career, your side projects, or your volunteer work, find something that gives you a sense of purpose. It's not just about making money—it's about making a difference.

5. **Build a Support System** : Surround yourself with people who support your goals and understand your values. Whether it's friends, family, or mentors, having a strong support system can help you stay grounded when things get tough.

As Gen Z, we're redefining what success looks like. It's no longer just about climbing the corporate ladder or earning a steady paycheck. Instead, we're focused on flexibility, purpose, and making an impact. We're blazing our own trails, challenging the status quo, and creating new paths to success. And while it's not always easy, I truly believe that our generation has the potential to change the world.

EIGHT

RELATIONSHIP

How can relationships **not** be included in a book about Gen Z, written by a Gen Z? After all, we're the most talked-about generation when it comes to relationships, right? We've been labeled the "**badnaam**" generation when it comes to dating, often asked: From what age did you get a boyfriend or girlfriend? It feels like people think we've rewritten the relationship rulebook, but in reality, we're just playing the game with new tools and challenges.

I'll be honest: I've become somewhat of a "relationship guru" among my friends. It's not because I've had a lot of relationships myself, but because my social circle is full of people with a wide range of love stories, heartbreaks, and complications. I've given advice, solved issues, and yes..... been dead wrong more than a few times. That's the thing, though. No one can truly master relationships because they're so complex. Especially when it comes to understanding the opposite gender, trust me, that's an entirely different ball game!

When I think about Gen Z and relationships, I don't feel like we're that experimental. Sure, some of us may dabble in multiple relationships, but for a lot of us, it's about forming deeper connections with one or two people. Millennials? They were the explorers, they experimented, dated around, tried to figure out what they wanted. Gen Z? We're all about the **vibe**. If your vibe matches mine, we're in. And the moment that vibe is off, it's over. It's almost like we're loyal to the idea of the relationship itself, even if the person we're with might not be 100% right for us. Surprisingly, despite the barrage of social media and platforms that make it easy to cheat or move on quickly, I think Gen Z is more grounded in relationships than we get credit for. Stats back this up. Data shows that we tend to stick with longer relationships compared to millennials. Maybe it's because we've grown up with technology that blurs boundaries, or maybe because we know how difficult it is to find someone who truly vibes with us.

Let's talk about how we form relationships in the first place. For Gen Z, it's all happening online. We've turned social media into the ultimate dating playground. Apps like Tinder, Bumble, and Hinge aren't just tools they're an expectation. Meeting someone the old-fashioned way feels like a novelty now. We don't just rely on these apps to find people; we use them to shape the very expectations of what a relationship should be.

Here's the tricky part: how do you take an online connection and make it real? It's one thing to exchange texts and emojis, but meeting in person can be nerve-wracking. Suddenly, you have to match the persona you've carefully curated online. No more filters, no more rehearsed replies. It's all raw and real and that's terrifying for many of us.

Gen Z also faces modern relationship phenomena that previous generations never dealt with. Ghosting, breadcrumbing, orbiting... these are terms we know too well. And they all come from the digital space, where it's too easy to vanish, string someone along, or stay in their life from a distance. Relationships that start online often end with a simple block or an unfollow. It's quick and ruthless, much like the world we've grown up in.

Commitment vs. Casual Connections

Then there's the question of commitment. We're living in the era of **situationships**, where no one wants to define what they have, but everyone wants something meaningful. It's almost paradoxical. On one hand, we're fiercely independent, valuing our space and freedom. On the other hand, we're emotional creatures who crave deep, genuine connections.

So why do we avoid labels? Because FOMO isn't just about events or opportunities it seeps into our relationships. What if committing to one person means we're missing out on someone better? What if, by defining things, we're locking ourselves into something that won't serve us in the long run? These questions loom large in Gen Z's collective psyche, making us hesitant to fully dive into commitment.

We've redefined what a relationship looks like. For some, it's perfectly normal to keep things casual for months, even years. For others, the desire to form a meaningful, committed bond is strong. But balancing these two impulses independence and connection creates a constant internal tug-of-war.

Let's be real—social media is both a blessing and a curse when it comes to relationships. On one hand, it helps us connect with people we might have never met otherwise. On the other hand, it sets impossible standards. We're constantly bombarded with images of "perfect" couples, aesthetically pleasing dates, and idealized moments that make our own relationships feel...well, less. The need for validation, for likes, for approval—this plays into how we view ourselves and our relationships. How many of us have posted a cute picture with our partner, only to obsess over how many likes it gets? And if it doesn't get enough, do we start questioning the relationship itself?

I've seen friends struggle with this. One day, they're fine with their partner, but the next, after scrolling through Instagram, they start feeling insecure. "Why doesn't my relationship look like that?" they wonder. And that's the trap—we start comparing, and in that comparison, we lose the real essence of the connection. Don't show to others, nazar lag jayegi.

Trust Issues in the Age of Screens

Trust is tricky in any relationship, but for Gen Z, it's complicated by the digital age. When you're always online, it's hard not to feel like you have to constantly prove your loyalty. We've all had moments of jealousy.... seeing our partner like someone's picture, comment on a post, or follow a new account. It sounds petty, but in a world where online presence is everything, these small actions can feel huge. There's also the issue of transparency. Being connected 24/7 means you're expected to share everything. Where are you? Who are you with? Why didn't you respond? It's exhausting, and it chips away at the foundation of trust. Sometimes, I think we trust less, not more, because we have so much access to each other's lives. The constant visibility creates this strange form of digital jealousy, making relationships even harder to navigate.

That's just the beginning of how Gen Z is navigating relationships in the digital age. We're trying to figure it all out how to love, trust, and connect in a world where the rules have changed. And while we're still learning, one thing's for sure: relationships today are more complex than ever before.

When discussing Gen Z and relationships, it's important to address those who aren't in relationships. In our fast-paced, digital world, not everyone is actively dating or in a committed relationship, but that doesn't mean they're untouched by the complexity of romantic and emotional experiences. In fact, those without relationships often face a different set of challenges, many of which revolve around self-satisfaction, loneliness, and the pressures of modern life.

In a generation where instant gratification is expected, it's no surprise that **self-satisfaction** (often in the form of self-help, without explicitly naming it) has become more prevalent. With the availability of adult content online and the ease of accessing it at any moment, this has become an outlet for many who are single, anxious, or even just seeking comfort in a world that often feels overwhelming. This trend isn't just about sexual release. It's about filling a void that might otherwise be filled by emotional connection or intimacy with another person. For some, it becomes a way to cope with stress, anxiety, or loneliness. However, the over-reliance on self-satisfaction can lead to its own set of problems. For one, it can create a cycle of dependence, where real-life relationships feel less exciting or fulfilling compared to the instant pleasure of what's available online.

Moreover, the constant consumption of adult content has undoubtedly sparked an increase in self-help habits. Reels, TikToks, and short-form video content often serve as distractions but can also fuel unhealthy obsessions. The cycle is vicious: you scroll through your feed, lose focus, and then indulge in content that diverts your mind temporarily, but leaves you feeling empty in the long run. For many, this isn't just an occasional indulgence; it becomes an addiction, which not only affects mental health but also one's ability to form real, meaningful relationships.

This growing phenomenon is something unique to Gen Z. In previous generations, such content was less accessible. Today, it's at our fingertips, feeding into our need for quick gratification, but at the same time pulling us away from genuine connection. Gen Z is rewriting the playbook when it comes to gender roles and romantic relationships. There is a newfound openness towards exploring gender identities and relationships that don't fit into the traditional heterosexual mold. Many of my friends, for example, are fluid in their expression of gender or identify as part of the LGBTQ+ community. What's fascinating is that, for Gen Z, this exploration doesn't carry the stigma that it might have in previous generations. We're open, accepting, and curious.

This fluidity extends to romantic relationships as well. Polyamory, open relationships, and non-monogamous setups are no longer taboo. They're seen as valid choices for individuals who feel that love and commitment don't have to be confined to just one person. I know people who are exploring multiple romantic partners, and it's not seen as scandalous—it's just another way of living and loving. But I don't feel it's correct as a sense of responsibility and care comes out of only one true relationship.

This openness has led to a more inclusive, diverse landscape of relationships. However, it's not without its challenges. Navigating fluidity means dealing with insecurities, managing boundaries, and learning new ways to communicate. It's not as simple as it looks on the surface. The complexity of emotions remains the same, if not heightened, in these setups.

But one thing is clear: Gen Z is pushing boundaries beyond the traditional models of relationships and not options like millennials. We have different cuisine to try from and millennials had multiple dishes, got the difference? We're not afraid to challenge societal norms, and in doing so, we're redefining what love, connection, and companionship mean.

Another significant challenge for Gen Z in relationships is the balancing act between family values and individual autonomy. Many of us come from families with traditional expectations find a stable partner, settle down, have kids. For those from conservative cultural backgrounds, like myself, there's an added layer of pressure to adhere to certain norms when it comes to relationships. But Gen Z is fiercely independent. We value our autonomy and often want to carve out our own paths. This creates tension between what our families expect from us and what we want for ourselves. Some of my friends have faced dilemmas..... whether to pursue relationships with partners that their families might not approve of, or to prioritize their own happiness over family expectations.

It's hard to strike this balance. Do you follow your heart, or do you respect your family's wishes? Many of us are navigating this tricky terrain, and it's not always easy to find a middle ground. We value our goals, dreams, and ambitions, but we also don't want to completely disregard the traditions and values that shaped us. For many, it's a constant push and pull, trying to satisfy both sides.

So, what does the future hold for relationships in a Gen Z world? As we grow older, our current relationship norms are likely to evolve. We might start to value more traditional forms of commitment, or we might continue to experiment with the boundaries of love and connection.

Technology is sure to play an even bigger role in shaping the future of relationships. Already, we're seeing the rise of virtual relationships, with people forming emotional bonds with AI companions. As AI and VR technologies advance, it's possible that relationships won't even require a human partner. Virtual reality could create immersive dating experiences, allowing people to "meet" without ever leaving their homes.

But while technology is shaping how we connect, it's also important to remember the fundamental human desire for intimacy, connection, and understanding. Even as we embrace new tools and platforms, the essence of relationships, the need to be seen, heard, and loved remains unchanged. We are, after all, social creatures. And while our methods of forming and maintaining relationships may change, that core desire for connection will never go away. It's possible that as we continue to evolve, we'll find a balance between technology and human touch, between independence and commitment, and between experimentation and stability. Gen Z is in the midst of a relationship revolution. From digital dependency and the rise of self-satisfaction, to evolving gender roles and the tension between family and individual values, we're navigating a world that's vastly different from that of previous generations. As we look to the future, the question remains: how will we continue to define love, connection, and intimacy in this ever-changing, fast-paced world?

This chapter delves into the complexities of relationships in the digital age, and as we continue to evolve, one thing is certain.... Gen Z will keep pushing boundaries, redefining norms, and shaping the future of how we love.

NINE

FIRE WITHIN

There's no denying that Gen Z carries a unique fire within them. This isn't necessarily the kind of fire that's visible through physical exertion or athletic prowess, but rather a burning mental energy. It's the kind of internal drive that makes Gen Z stand out from the rest of the generations before them. They are the generation of creators, disruptors, and innovators with constantly on the move mentally, with an unrelenting thirst for more.

This fire is what drives them to tackle societal norms, question the status quo, and carve out their own identity in a fast-paced, ever-evolving world. This generation is often misunderstood as being distracted, but in reality, their minds are simply running at a higher frequency. This mental fire can be a double-edged sword on one hand, it fuels creativity and ambition, while on the other, if not properly channeled, it can lead to burnout or anxiety.

I remember when my school principal would often pull me aside and say, "Mahboob, you need to channel your energy in a better manner." Back then, I didn't fully grasp the depth of his words. Like many others from my generation, I had a surplus of mental energy, constantly racing with ideas, ambitions, and goals, but struggled to focus that energy into productive channels. It wasn't until much later that I understood the importance of harnessing this fire, rather than letting it consume me.

The Rise of Gen Z Influencers: Mental Energy at Work

One of the clearest reflections of this mental energy can be seen in the world of influencers. Gen Z influencers, unlike the ones from previous generations, aren't just about superficial content; they are leveraging their platforms to share ideas, spread social awareness, and bring about change. They are the embodiment of how this internal fire, when properly harnessed, can inspire and impact millions.

Take, for example, **Emma Chamberlain**, a 22-year-old content creator who revolutionized YouTube with her candid, raw approach. Emma's content is not the typical curated, polished videos we've grown accustomed to. Instead, she represents a shift towards authenticity, often talking about mental health, the pressures of social media, and the struggles of being young in an unpredictable world. Despite her casual and laid-back approach, her videos show a strong sense of creative direction. She doesn't shy away from tough conversations, and in doing so, has built a community of millions who relate to her experiences.

Another shining example is **Greta Thunberg**, the young environmental activist who, at just 15, began her school strike for climate. She may not have the glamorous life of a traditional influencer, but her mental focus, conviction, and determination to fight for climate action have made her a global icon. Greta's fire for environmental change is a clear reflection of how Gen Z's mental energy can be directed towards a cause greater than themselves. Her ability to stay focused and channel her fire has rallied millions of people, young and old, to pay attention to the climate crisis.

These influencers aren't just using their platforms to entertain; they are using them to challenge the way we think, question societal norms, and push for change. The mental energy of Gen Z is not idle—it's productive, and when funneled in the right direction, it can move mountains.

Channeling the Mental Fire: Lessons I've Learned

While this internal drive is a powerful tool, it can easily spiral out of control if not channeled properly. This is where my principal's advice truly came into play. He used to remind me that energy, whether physical or mental, is a resource. It's finite, and it must be directed with purpose if you want to see results.

Here are a few key strategies I learned for channeling this fire better, strategies that I think will be invaluable for anyone from Gen Z struggling with the same:

1. Prioritize Your Focus

With so much mental energy, it's tempting to try and do everything at once. You'll want to start multiple projects, pursue various interests, and consume vast amounts of information. But as I learned, this can quickly lead to burnout. Instead, it's important to focus on what truly matters at the moment. Break down your big ideas into smaller, manageable tasks and focus on one at a time. Your mental energy is like a laser when it's scattered, it's weak, but when it's focused, it's powerful.

2. Take Breaks to Recharge

It may sound counterintuitive, but taking breaks is essential to sustaining mental energy. We live in a world that praises hustle culture, but mental rest is critical for longevity. My English teacher would always say, "Even the brightest flame needs time to burn slower." Regular breaks not only help prevent burnout but also give your mind time to process information, leading to greater creativity when you return to your tasks.

3. Find Your Passion and Dive Deep

The fire within Gen Z is most visible when it's fueled by passion. Whether it's climate activism, entrepreneurship, content creation, or another area, finding your true passion and diving deep into it will help you direct your energy more effectively. When you're genuinely interested in something, you'll naturally want to dedicate more time and effort to it. But remember, passion doesn't always equate to immediate success it requires patience and perseverance.

4. Build a Routine

One of the best ways to channel your mental energy is to build a routine. It provides structure and allows you to focus on what's important without getting overwhelmed. My father taught me that consistency is key. No matter how chaotic your mind feels, following a routine helps stabilize your day and channels that mental fire into productive outcomes.

5. Surround Yourself with Positive Energy

The people you surround yourself with can either fuel your fire or extinguish it. Positive, driven people can help inspire you and keep you motivated. In contrast, those who drain your energy with negativity can make it harder to maintain focus. I've learned to be selective about my inner circle.... people who inspire me, push me to think differently, and support my ideas are the ones I keep close.

6. Turn Ideas into Action

Having mental energy often means having a surplus of ideas. But ideas alone won't get you anywhere. It's essential to turn those ideas into actionable steps. My father say, "**Ideas are just potential**; action makes them real." I learned to turn my mental fire into real-world outcomes by focusing on execution. Start small, and gradually you'll see your ideas take shape.

The mental energy that defines Gen Z is both a blessing and a challenge. When used wisely, it can lead to incredible innovation, creativity, and change, as we've seen with influencers and leaders in the generation. However, without proper focus and channeling, this energy can also lead to confusion, frustration, and burnout.

As I reflect on the lessons from my principal and the incredible influencers of my generation, I realize that our fire is a gift, but it must be respected. We need to learn how to manage it, direct it, and use it to bring about the world we envision. This chapter is not just about recognizing the energy inside us but about learning how to make the most of it, not just for ourselves but for the future of the world.

In the first part of this chapter, we explored the undeniable mental energy that defines Gen Z, how it manifests in creativity and disruption, and the importance of channeling it productively. Let's look into specific examples from Indian influencers who exemplify this fire, using their unique content styles to inspire millions and build movements of their own.

Apoorva: The Rebel Kid

Known as **The.rebel.kid** on social media, Apoorva is a true representative of the rebellious spirit of Gen Z. As her username suggests, she's not one to conform to societal norms. Whether it's her unapologetic fashion choices or her relatable, sarcastic humor, Apoorva is constantly pushing the boundaries and challenging expectations. Her content isn't just about fashion; it's about breaking free from the mold and encouraging her audience to do the same.

Her fashion videos stand out for their boldness—Apoorva isn't afraid to experiment with different styles, whether it's mixing high street with thrift, or pairing traditional Indian wear with edgy accessories. Through her bold statements, she communicates a powerful message: Be yourself, no matter what anyone says. In doing so, she inspires her audience to break away from societal pressures about how one should dress or act.

Apoorva's ability to relate to her audience on a personal level is key to her success. She uses humor to connect with her followers in an authentic and organic way. Through her funny videos, she highlights everyday struggles, be it with parents, friendships, or career expectations. Her humor is raw and unfiltered she doesn't sugarcoat the challenges of being young today, but instead embraces them, turning them into something laughable and relatable.

This kind of content is powerful because it reflects the mindset of the average Gen Z individual: we are tired of living within pre-set boundaries. There is a deep desire to break free from the stereotypes and limitations imposed by previous generations. Apoorva's videos are a call to arms for her followers to express their true selves without shame, to rebel against the outdated norms that no longer serve them, and to embrace the fluidity of identity.

Her content shows how Gen Z, far from being apathetic or disinterested, is a generation that is quietly rebellious. We may not always stage protests or organize movements in the streets, but we resist conformity through the choices we make to be it in fashion, relationships, or career paths. For Gen Z, rebellion is a form of self-expression. We challenge norms simply by being who we are.

Agasthya Shah: Building the **#AgFam**

Another rising star among Indian Gen Z influencers is Agasthya Shah, a 20-year-old content creator who is well on his way to building an empire of his own—lovingly referred to as the #AgFam by his loyal followers. What makes Agasthya's content stand out is the fact that he, like many in Gen Z, is not afraid to use humor as a tool to make serious points.

Agasthya creates short, punchy, and hilarious videos that often revolve around the quirks of being young in India. From relatable skits about school life to poking fun at the awkwardness of teenage years, Agasthya knows how to tap into the everyday experiences of Gen Z. His content is quick to consume but leaves a lasting impact because it reflects the reality of growing up in a fast-paced, hyperconnected world.

One of the reasons why Agasthya's content resonates so well with his audience is because he never takes himself too seriously. While previous generations may have focused on showcasing perfection whether in careers, family life, or relationships also Agasthya embodies the idea that it's okay to be messy, to make mistakes, and to laugh at yourself along the way. His content doesn't strive for an unattainable ideal; instead, it celebrates the chaos and imperfection that comes with youth.

Agasthya's #AgFam isn't just a fanbase, it's a community. He engages with his followers on a personal level, often asking for their input on his content and creating videos based on their suggestions. This type of engagement isn't just about building numbers; it's about creating a sense of belonging. For a generation that often feels isolated or disconnected, the #AgFam offers a safe space where young people can feel seen and understood.

This highlights another important aspect of the Gen Z mindset: we are not just passive consumers of content; we actively seek out spaces where we can contribute, engage, and belong. Social media has given Gen Z a platform not only to express themselves but also to find communities of like-minded individuals. For Agasthya, content creation is more than just entertainment it's about creating connections and fostering a sense of solidarity among his followers.

The Mindset Behind Their Success

Both Apoorva and Agasthya showcase different facets of the Gen Z mindset, but there are key commonalities that explain why they've been able to build such strong followings:

1. **Authenticity**: Gen Z has an inherent distrust of anything that feels fake or forced. Influencers like Apoorva and Agasthya thrive because they come across as real people, not as manufactured personalities. They are honest about their struggles, their imperfections, and their journeys, which makes them relatable to their audience.

2. **Relatability**: One of the reasons why these influencers have gained such immense popularity is because their content reflects the realities of the everyday Gen Z experience. Whether it's Apoorva's rebellious fashion choices or Agasthya's comedic take on awkward teenage moments, their content resonates because it mirrors the lives of their followers.

3. **Community Building**: Both Apoorva and Agasthya have built communities around their content. They don't just broadcast their ideas to the world; they engage with their followers, listen to their feedback, and make them feel like they are part of something bigger. For a generation that is constantly seeking connection, this sense of community is invaluable.

4. **Breaking Boundaries**: Gen Z isn't afraid to challenge societal norms, and that's a key part of what makes influencers like Apoorva and Agasthya so appealing. They encourage their followers to think outside the box, to question traditional ways of doing things, and to carve out their own paths. Whether it's Apoorva's rejection of conventional fashion or Agasthya's irreverent humor, these influencers exemplify the rebellious spirit of Gen Z.

Channeling the Fire: How to Focus Your Mental Energy

While Apoorva and Agasthya represent the success that can come from channeling Gen Z's mental fire into creative outlets, not everyone has mastered this art. As I mentioned earlier, my school principal's advice about channeling my energy in a better way has stuck with me for years, and I've learned a few key strategies that can help anyone—whether you're an aspiring influencer, an entrepreneur, or just someone trying to make sense of life as a young adult.

1. Identify Your Passion

The first step to channeling your mental energy is figuring out what drives you. Both Apoorva and Agasthya found their passion in content creation, but that doesn't mean everyone needs to be an influencer. Maybe your passion lies in activism, entrepreneurship, technology, or the arts. Whatever it is, identifying it early allows you to focus your energy on something that genuinely excites and motivates you.

2. Set Clear Goals

Once you've identified your passion, it's important to set clear, achievable goals. This helps you avoid feeling overwhelmed by the sheer amount of mental energy you have. For example, if your goal is to start a YouTube channel like Agasthya, break it down into smaller steps: decide on your niche, plan your content, and set a schedule for posting videos. By having a clear roadmap, you can focus your energy more effectively.

2. **Embrace Imperfection**

One of the biggest lessons I've learned from watching influencers like Apoorva and Agasthya is that perfection is overrated. Gen Z doesn't need things to be polished or flawless we appreciate raw, real content. So, don't be afraid to put yourself out there, even if things aren't perfect. Whether you're starting a business, launching a project, or simply expressing yourself online, remember that it's better to take action and learn from your mistakes than to wait for everything to be perfect.

4. **Stay Consistent**

While passion and creativity are important, consistency is what truly leads to success. Both Apoorva and Agasthya post content regularly, engage with their audience frequently, and continue to evolve their platforms over time. Consistency doesn't mean you need to be perfect every day, but it does mean showing up and putting in the effort, even when you don't feel like it.

5. **Surround Yourself with Support**

Finally, one of the most important lessons I've learned is the value of surrounding yourself with supportive people. Just like Apoorva and Agasthya have built strong communities around their content, it's important to have a support system in your personal life that believes in you and encourages you to keep going. Whether it's friends, family, or mentors, having people who uplift you can make all the difference.

The fire inside Gen Z is a powerful force one that has the potential to change the world. Whether you're creating content like Apoorva and Agasthya, starting your own business, or pursuing a personal passion, the key is learning how to channel that energy in a way that's productive and fulfilling. The mental fire of Gen Z is both a gift and a challenge, and the more we learn to harness it, the more we can

TEN

IN PROCESS

As we come to the end of this book, I find myself at a crossroads. How can I sum up a generation that's still evolving, still figuring out its place in the world? The truth is, the story of Gen Z is far from complete. We're in a constant state of transition, moving between worlds old and new, traditional and progressive, digital and real. And maybe, just maybe, that's the beauty of it.

We haven't yet been proven to be the best or the worst generation, as some might claim. We're not a finished product, and that's okay. We're learning, growing, and navigating this incredibly fast-paced, chaotic, and ever-changing world. We've been misunderstood at times, praised at others, but what stands out most is that we are writing our own stories, in our own way. Every decision we make, every challenge we face, is shaping the future not only for ourselves but for the world around us.

But this book isn't just about my story or my perspective as a Gen Z. It's about **you**. Whether you are a Gen Z reading this or someone from a different generation looking in, this book was always meant to be a conversation or a way to connect, to bridge the gap between our experiences, and to understand each other better.

So here's my question to you: What does being Gen Z mean to you?

If you're part of this generation, how do you see yourself in the chapters I've written? Do you relate to the struggles, the triumphs, the fears, and the hopes? Have you felt the impatience, the restlessness, and the desire to change the world in a way that only we seem to? Maybe your story is different, and maybe that's the whole point .... we are a generation defined by our individuality, but bound together by our shared experience of growing up in this whirlwind of technology, social change, and shifting values. If you're from a different generation, how do you see us? Do you recognize your own experiences in ours, or does it feel foreign, like looking at life through a completely different lens? What have you learned about Gen Z that you didn't know before? And how do you think we, as a generation, will shape the world in the years to come?

This book was never meant to be a finished product. It's a reflection of a journey....... journey that's still ongoing, still full of unanswered questions and paths yet to be explored. So, I invite you to complete it. Take a moment to reflect on your own experiences, your own thoughts about what it means to be Gen Z, or to witness Gen Z's journey from the outside. Write the last chapter of this book in your own words. Let your thoughts, your insights, and your perspectives be the final version of this story.

Because this book is dedicated to you. To all of us, really. It's a shared story, one that we are all writing together, one moment, one experience, one decision at a time.

I hope, in these pages, you found something that resonated with you, that made you think or feel or even question. I hope you laughed, nodded in agreement, or maybe even shook your head in disagreement. But most of all, I hope you found yourself here, in some small way, because that's what this was always meant to be a mirror reflecting the pulse of a generation that's still beating, still growing, still moving forward.

So, what's next for us? Only time will tell. But one thing is for sure: the story of Gen Z is far from over, and I can't wait to see how it unfolds with all of us, together, writing the next chapter.

With all my heart, thank you for being a part of this journey.

Call For Action

As you reach the end, I want to extend my deepest gratitude to you for taking the time to read and engage with these thoughts, experiences, and reflections. This journey has been about more than just understanding the challenges that come with growing up in a rapidly changing world—it's about starting a conversation. A conversation that acknowledges the struggles, celebrates the victories, and explores new ways to navigate the dynamic landscape we all find ourselves in.

But this isn't where the dialogue ends—it's where it begins. If you've resonated with any part of this book, if you've faced similar challenges, or even if you just want to share your own story, I'd love to hear from you. Let's continue this conversation, because your voice matters.

You can connect with me through my website at **www.mahboobalam.org**

Scan

Whether you have questions, need advice, or simply want to chat about life, I'm here. This platform is a space where we can keep exploring the Gen Z journey together, helping each other grow and learn along the way.

We're all in this together—connected by our shared experiences, struggles, and hopes. Let's keep the conversation going. I look forward to hearing from you!

Additional Resources

For those interested in exploring more about the topics discussed in this book, I recommend the following resources:

1. Generation Z Unfiltered (by Riya Goel)
2. What is Gen Z (McKinsey & Company)
3. The Private Life of Generation Z (by David Atkins)
4. You or your Gen Z subordinate

Lift above and Live above

They Have To Say

In an attempt to capture a balanced view of what older generations think about Gen Z, I conducted interviews with 10 individuals—five Millennials and five from Gen X. Their insights were fascinating, shedding light on how these generations perceive us and, in some ways, challenge us to reflect on our strengths and weaknesses. I merged their feedback into a cohesive testimonial, with the help of ChatGPT, to present a unified perspective from both generations.

Millennials' Perspective on Gen Z

Millennials, typically born between the early 1980s and mid-2000s, expressed a mix of admiration and concern regarding Gen Z. They see us as highly aspirational individuals, always aiming to excel in our careers and pushing boundaries in ways they did not feel were possible at our age. One millennial remarked, "Gen Z is highly driven. They don't just want to follow traditional paths; they want to carve their own. They are always chasing success."

However, the Millennials also pointed out that Gen Z tends to be overconfident at times. We are seen as a generation that takes risks and often "jumps in" without a plan, compared to their more structured approach to life and career. According to them, this can be a double-edged sword. As one Millennial shared, "While it's inspiring to see how Gen Z leaps into new projects without fear, they sometimes overlook the importance of planning and preparation."

Many Millennials feel that Gen Z doesn't always recognize the weight of the opportunities we have. We are viewed as a generation that, at times, takes things for granted—be it resources, technology, or the freedom to explore new possibilities. But they balance this critique with acknowledgment that we are genuinely concerned about our future and the state of the world. One interviewee said, "I see the anxiety in Gen Z about what's coming next, especially around job security and the environment. They're worried, but it doesn't always show because they act confidently."

Millennials appreciate our optimism and forward-thinking mindset, but they believe we could benefit from integrating some of their approach to planning and critical thinking before diving into new ventures.

Gen X's Perspective on Gen Z

Gen X group, born between the mid-1960s and early 1980s, expressed a different, and perhaps more empathetic, view of Gen Z. They emphasized our creativity and our willingness to take new approaches, admiring how we're constantly thinking outside the box. Gen X, having witnessed rapid changes in technology and society, respects how Gen Z adapts to these shifts and innovates. One Gen X respondent noted, "Gen Z is incredibly innovative. They aren't afraid to challenge the status quo and come up with new ways of doing things, whether in work, life, or social issues."

However, they also pointed out a key area where Gen Z can improve: patience. Gen X believes that while we have the potential to make a significant impact on the world, we often expect immediate results without putting in the long-term effort. A common refrain from the Gen X interviewees was, "Gen Z has all the tools, all the resources, but they need to learn patience. Things don't happen overnight, and sometimes, you need to slow down to truly excel."

Interestingly, many from Gen X believe that, while Millennials might be more practical, Gen Z is more emotionally sound. They argue that we're more in touch with our feelings and are more open about mental health, which makes us better equipped to handle emotional challenges. One Gen X individual said, "I think Gen Z is far more emotionally intelligent than we were at that age. They talk about mental health, express their feelings openly, and aren't afraid to seek help when they need it."

This emotional intelligence, combined with our creativity and adaptability, leads many from Gen X to feel optimistic about the future in our hands. They see Gen Z as a generation that, once we learn to temper our impatience and build on our emotional strengths, could truly make the world a better place.

How I Compiled These Insights

To write this section, I conducted interviews with 10 individuals across two generational groups—Millennials and Gen X. I intentionally chose five people from each group to ensure I could capture a well-rounded view of what they think about Gen Z. Their feedback was raw and detailed, filled with both compliments and critiques.

Interestingly, the responses were not far off from what I expected. As a member of Gen Z, I'm acutely aware of both our strengths and our weaknesses, and these testimonials reinforced that view. Millennials admire our ambition but question our impulsiveness, while Gen X appreciates our creativity and emotional depth but advises patience.

Ultimately, both generations believe in our potential. Their critiques are meant to guide us toward growth, not hinder our confidence. These testimonials reflect the fact that, while Gen Z is breaking new ground, we have a lot to learn from those who came before us. Their experiences offer valuable lessons that can help us temper our boldness with wisdom and build a better future—not just for ourselves but for the generations that will follow.